Patchwork
Comforters, Throws & Quilts™

Edited By Jeanne Stauffer & Sandra L. Hatch

HOUSE of
WHITE
BIRCHES

PUBLISHERS
SINCE 1947

Patchwork
Comforters, Throws & Quilts™

JW

Editors **Jeanne Stauffer & Sandra L. Hatch**
Art Director **Brad Snow**
Publishing Services Director **Brenda Gallmeyer**

Assistant Editor **Erika Mann**
Editorial Assistant **Kortney Barile**
Assistant Art Director **Nick Pierce**
Copy Supervisor **Michelle Beck**
Copy Editors **Angie Buckles, Mary O'Donnell, Amanda Scheerer**
Technical Artist **Connie Rand**

Graphic Arts Supervisor **Ronda Bechinski**
Book Design **Brad Snow**
Graphic Artists **Debby Keel, Erin Augsburger**
Production Assistants **Marj Morgan**

Photography Supervisor **Tammy Christian**
Photography **Matthew Owen**
Photo Stylist **Tammy Steiner**

Printed in China
Library of Congress Number: 2009921059
Hardcover ISBN: 978-1-59217-259-7
Softcover ISBN: 978-1-59217-260-3

DRGbooks.com

1 2 3 4 5 6 7 8 9

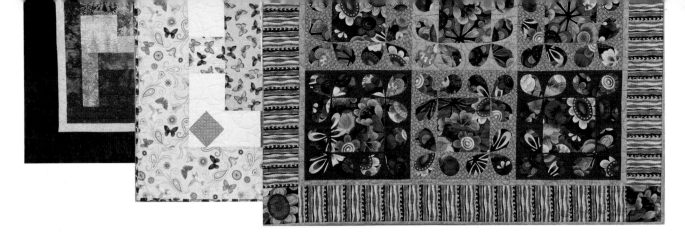

Welcome

To many people, the words patchwork and quilts are synonymous. They both bring to mind bed quilts that are large enough to fit a full-size bed. Quilters know that isn't always the case. Quilts come in a wide variety of sizes and shapes, as you will discover when you look at the scrumptious projects in this book.

To start things off, the first chapter has all quilt runners. These quilts are long and narrow—just right for placing across the end of the bed or for wrapping around your shoulders when you need a little comfort. They bring Simple Comforts to those who use them.

The designs in the second chapter use convenient precut rolls or squares of fabric instead of the traditional patches cut from yardage. These Rolls & Squares throws are easier and faster to complete than an ordinary quilt; they're just right for beginners or for those short on time.

Traditionally quilts were made in blocks, but that has changed with the designs in the Uncommon Quilts chapter. In some cases, the entire quilt is one block. Or the blocks are off-center, giving the quilt a very unique look. These quilts are still patchwork; they just look a little unusual.

Although patchwork reigns supreme in the mind of most quilters, appliqué is becoming more popular. Patchwork is still the primary technique used in the Patchwork Plus chapter, but all of the designs also use at least a touch of appliqué.

There are certain quilt designs that experienced quilters recognize. The projects in The New Classic chapter use these familiar blocks, but they add a few twists and turns, so you may need to take a second look to see the original familiar block. If you like the traditional, you'll love the projects in this chapter.

Patchwork quilts are for babies also. Stitched with care, the quilts in the Baby Hugs chapter all say, "I love you."

Whatever kind of patchwork you enjoy, we wish you hours of pleasurable quilting as you stitch the projects in this book!

Happy quilting,

Jeanne Stauffer   *Sandra L. Hatch*

Contents

Simple Comforts

Long, narrow quilts are the latest in quilting. Placed at the end of a bed, they become foot warmers while adding a quick-to-make decorative touch to any bedroom. They are also the perfect size and shape for wrapping around yourself in those moments when you need a little comfort.

Bed of Roses

This pretty bed warmer will add a bit of cheer and color to any bedroom.

Design by **JULIE WEAVER**

PROJECT SPECIFICATIONS

Skill Level: Intermediate
Quilt Size: 79" x 39"
Block Size: 8" x 8"
Number of Blocks: 12

MATERIALS

- ⅛ yard red mottled
- ⅓ yard red tonal 1
- ¾ yard cream tonal
- ¾ yard green tonal
- ⅞ yard green small floral
- 1 yard red tonal 2
- 1⅛ yards green large floral
- Batting 85" x 45"
- Backing 85" x 45"
- Neutral-color all-purpose thread
- Quilting thread
- Basic sewing tools and supplies

Cutting

1. Cut one 2½" by fabric width A strip red mottled.

2. Cut three 2½" by fabric width strips cream tonal; set aside one strip for A-B strip set. Subcut remaining strips into (12) 4½" C pieces.

3. Cut three 4½" by fabric width strips cream tonal; subcut strips into (24) 4½" J squares.

4. Cut four 2½" by fabric width strips red tonal 2; subcut strips into (12) 4½" D pieces and (12) 6½" E pieces.

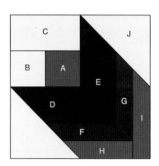

Rose
8" x 8" Block
Make 12

5. Cut (10) 2" by fabric width O/P/S/T strips red tonal 2.

6. Cut five 1½" by fabric width strips red tonal 1; subcut strips into (12) 6½" F pieces and (12) 7½" G pieces.

7. Cut six 1½" by fabric width strips green tonal; subcut strips into (12) 7½" H pieces and (12) 8½" I pieces.

8. Cut five 2½" by fabric width strips green tonal; subcut strips into (10) 18½" M strips and three 2½" K squares.

9. Cut four 2½" by fabric width strips green small floral; subcut strips into (12) 8½" L strips and eight 2½" N squares.

10. Cut six 2¼" by fabric width binding strips green small floral.

11. Cut five 4½" by fabric width Q/R strips green large floral.

12. Cut six 2" by fabric width U/V strips green large floral.

Completing the Blocks

Note: *Use a ¼" seam allowance throughout.*

1. Sew the A strip to the B strip with right sides together along length; press seam toward the A strip.

2. Subcut the A-B strip set into (12) 2½" A-B units as shown in Figure 1.

Figure 1

3. Sew C to one A-B unit as shown in Figure 2; press seam toward C.

Figure 2

4. Add D–I in alphabetical order to one side and then the adjacent side referring to Figure 3 for placement; press seams toward newly added strip after each stitching.

Figure 3

5. Draw a diagonal line from corner to corner on the wrong side of each J square.

6. Place a J square right sides together on opposite corners of the stitched unit and stitch on the marked line as shown in Figure 4; trim seam to ¼" and press J to the right side to complete one Rose block, again referring to Figure 4.

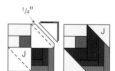

Figure 4

7. Repeat steps 3–6 to complete 12 Rose blocks.

Completing the Top

1. Join two Rose blocks with an L strip as shown in Figure 5; press seams toward the L strip. Repeat to make six L/block units.

Figure 5

2. Sew K between two L strips; press seams toward L. Repeat to make three K-L units.

3. Join two L/block units with one K-L unit to make a four-block unit as shown in Figure 6; press seams toward the K-L unit. Repeat to make three four-block units.

Figure 6

4. Join the four-block units with four M strips; press seams toward M strips.

5. Join three M strips with four N squares to make a sashing strip as shown in Figure 7; press seams toward M strips. Repeat to make two sashing strips.

Figure 7

6. Sew a sashing strip to the top and bottom of the pieced section to complete the pieced center; press seams toward sashing strips.

7. Join the O/P/S/T strips on the short ends to make one long strip; subcut strip into two 25½" P strips, two 62½" O strips, two 73½" S strips and two 36½" T strips.

8. Sew the O strips to opposite long sides and P strips to the short ends of the pieced center; press seams toward O and P strips.

9. Repeat step 7 with Q and R strips, cutting two 65½" Q strips and two 33½" R strips.

10. Sew the S strips to opposite long sides and T strips to the short ends of the pieced center; press seams toward S and T strips.

11. Repeat step 7 with U and V strips, cutting two 76½" U strips and two 39½" T strips.

12. Sew U strips to opposite long sides and V strips to the short ends of the pieced center; press seams toward U and V strips to complete the top.

13. Layer, quilt and bind referring to Finishing Your Quilt on page 173. ✤

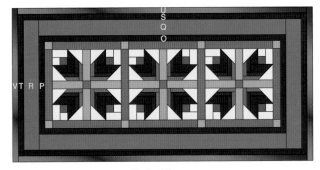

Bed of Roses
Placement Diagram 79" x 39"

Hexagon Beauty

Colorful 2½"-wide strips work perfectly in this comforter.

Design by **LUCY A. FAZELY & MICHAEL L. BURNS**

PROJECT SPECIFICATIONS

Skill Level: Beginner
Quilt Size: 76¾" x 28"
Block Size: 9¼" x 8"
Number of Blocks: 14

MATERIALS

- 7 each assorted light (A) and dark (B) 2½" x 42" strips
- ⅓ yard gold tonal
- ½ yard white tonal
- ⅝ yard black solid
- 1 yard large floral
- Batting 83" x 34"
- Backing 83" x 34"
- Neutral-color all-purpose thread
- Quilting thread
- Basic sewing tools and supplies

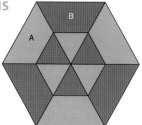

Hexagon Beauty
9¼" x 8" Block
Make 14

Cutting

1. Cut three 4½" by fabric width strips white tonal; use template A/B/C to cut 32 C triangles as shown in Figure 1.

Figure 1

2. Cut five 1½" by fabric width D/E strips gold tonal.

3. Cut five 5½" by fabric width F/G strips large floral.

4. Cut six 2¼" by fabric width strips black solid for binding.

Completing the Blocks

1. Select one each A and B strip; sew together along length with right sides together to make an A-B strip set; press seam toward B.

2. Place the A/B/C template on the strip, aligning the line on the template with the seam between the A and B strips as shown in Figure 2; cut one A-B unit. Turn the template and cut a B-A unit, again referring to Figure 2. Repeat to cut six each A-B and B-A units from the strip set.

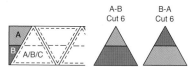

Figure 2

3. Join two B-A and one A-B unit to make half a block as shown in Figure 3; repeat with two A-B units and one B-A unit to complete the second half of the block, again referring to Figure 3. Press seams in each unit in one direction.

Figure 3

4. Join the half blocks to complete one Hexagon Beauty block referring to the block drawing; press seam in one direction.

5. Repeat steps 3 and 4 to complete an identical Hexagon Beauty block using the remaining A-B and B-A units.

6. Repeat steps 1–4 to complete seven sets of two matching Hexagon Beauty blocks to total 14 blocks.

Completing the Top

1. Sew C to opposite sides of each Hexagon Beauty block as shown in Figure 4; press seams toward C.

Figure 4

2. Join seven Hexagon Beauty/C units as shown in Figure 5 to make a row; press seams in one direction. Repeat to make two rows. Sew a C triangle to each end of each row, again referring to Figure 5; press seams toward C.

Figure 5

3. Trim the C triangles at the end of each row ¼" past the seam points to make straight side edges as shown in Figure 6.

¼"

Figure 6

4. Join the rows with seams going in opposite directions to complete the pieced center; press seams in one direction.

5. Join the D/E strips with right sides together on the short ends to make one long strip; press seams open.

Subcut the strip into two 16½" D strips and two 67¼" E strips.

6. Sew the D strips to opposite short ends and E strips to the long sides of the pieced center; press seams toward D and E strips.

7. Join the F/G strips with right sides together on the short ends to make one long strip; press seams open. Subcut the strip into two 18½" F strips and two 77¼" G strips.

8. Sew the F strips to opposite short ends and G strips to the long sides of the pieced center; press seams toward F and G strips to complete the pieced top. ❖

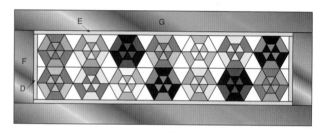

Hexagon Beauty
Placement Diagram 76¾" x 28"

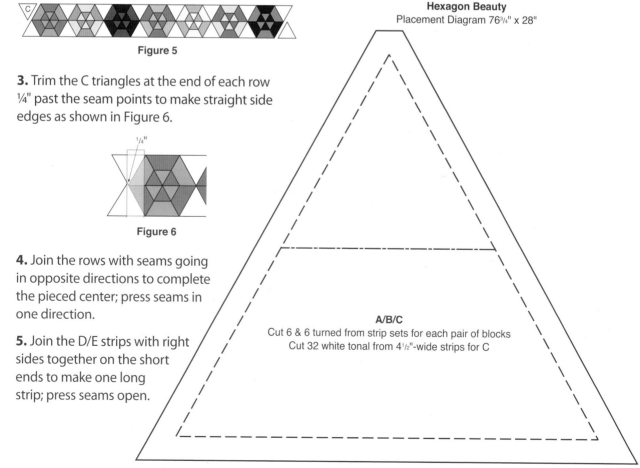

A/B/C
Cut 6 & 6 turned from strip sets for each pair of blocks
Cut 32 white tonal from 4½"-wide strips for C

Dust Storm Bed Warmer

Add a little extra warmth for your feet with this neutral-color bed warmer.

Design by **CONNIE KAUFFMAN**

Skill Level: Advanced
Quilt Size: 91" x 37½"
Block Size: 18½" x 18½"
Number of Blocks: 3

MATERIALS

- ¼ yard blue/gray print
- ⅜ yard tan floral dots
- ⅜ yard cream print
- ⅜ yard tan tonal
- ⅞ yard peach/tan print
- 1 yard gray tonal
- 1⅜ yards medium brown tonal
- 1½ yards dark brown tonal
- Batting 97" x 44"
- Backing 97" x 44"
- Neutral-color all-purpose thread
- Quilting thread
- Basic sewing tools and supplies

Cutting

***Note:** There are many pieces in this pattern; when cutting, keep like-pieces together in a labeled plastic zipper bag.*

1. Cut one 3⅝" by fabric width strip blue/gray print; subcut strip into eight 3⅝"

L squares and two 2⅝" x 2⅝" E squares. Cut each square in half on one diagonal to make four E triangles and 16 L triangles.

2. Cut two 4¼" by fabric width strips tan floral dots; subcut strip into (12) 4¼" F squares and two 2¼" x 2¼" M squares.

3. Cut two 3⅝" by fabric width strips medium brown tonal; subcut strips into (12) 3⅝" H squares; cut each square in half on one diagonal to make 24 H triangles.

4. Cut two 4⅝" by fabric width strips medium brown tonal; subcut strips into (12) 4⅝" I squares; cut each square in half on one diagonal to make 24 I triangles.

5. Cut four 3½" by fabric width V strips medium brown tonal.

6. Cut two 7¼" x 38" W strips medium brown tonal.

7. Cut two 4⅝" by fabric width strips tan tonal; subcut strips into (12) 4⅝" J squares and four 3⅝" x 3⅝" G squares; cut each square in half on one diagonal to make 24 J triangles and eight G triangles.

8. Cut one 3" by fabric width strip cream tonal; subcut strip into (10) 3" P squares.

9. Cut one 2⅝" by fabric width strip cream tonal; subcut strip into four 2⅝" K squares and two 2⅛" x 2⅛" D squares. Cut each D and K square in half on one diagonal to make four D and eight K triangles.

10. Cut one 2⅛" by fabric width strip gray tonal; subcut strip into (16) 2⅛" Q squares. Cut each square in half on one diagonal to make 32 Q triangles.

11. Cut four 2" by fabric width R strips gray tonal.

12. Cut two 2" x 29" S strips gray tonal.

13. Cut three 2⅝" by fabric width strips peach/tan print; subcut strips into (36) 2⅝" O squares. Cut each square in half on one diagonal to make 72 O triangles.

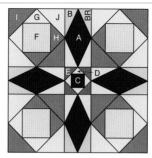
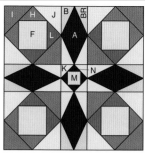

Dust Storm A
18½" x 18½" Block
Make 1

Dust Storm B
18½" x 18½" Block
Make 2

14. Cut one 2¼" by fabric width strip dark brown tonal; subcut strip into nine 2¼" C squares and four 2⅛" x 2⅛" N squares. Cut each N square in half on one diagonal to make eight N triangles.

15. Cut four 2" by fabric width T strips dark brown tonal.

16. Cut two 3" x 32" U strips dark brown tonal.

17. Cut seven 2¼" by fabric width strips dark brown tonal for binding.

18. Prepare templates for A and B using patterns given; cut as directed on each piece.

Completing the Blocks

Note: *Use a ¼" seam allowance throughout.*

1. Sew one each peach/tan B and BR and one each cream tonal B and BR to a dark brown A to make a brown A-B unit as shown in Figure 1; press seams away from A. Repeat to make 12 brown A-B units.

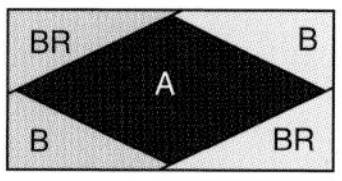

Figure 1 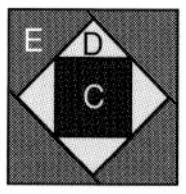   **Figure 2**

2. Sew D to each side of C; press seams toward D. Add E to each side of the C-D unit to complete a C-D-E unit as shown in Figure 2; press seams toward E.

3. Sew G to two sides and H to the remaining two sides of F; press seams toward G and H. Sew I to two sides and J to the remaining two sides of the

F-G-H unit to complete an H corner unit as shown in Figure 3. Repeat to make four H corner units.

Figure 3

Figure 4

4. Sew H to two sides and L to the remaining two sides of F; press seams toward H and L. Sew I to two sides and J to the remaining two sides of the F-H-L unit to complete an L corner unit as shown in Figure 4; repeat to make eight L corner units.

5. Sew N to each side of M; press seams toward N. Sew K to each side of the M-N unit to complete a K-M-N unit as shown in Figure 5; press seams toward K. Repeat to make two K-M-N units.

Figure 5

Figure 6

6. To complete the Dust Storm A block, sew a brown A-B unit to opposite sides of the C-D-E unit to make the center row as shown in Figure 6; press seams open.

7. Join two H corner units with a brown A-B unit to make the top row as shown in Figure 7; press seams open. Repeat to make the bottom row.

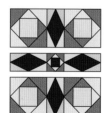

Figure 7   **Figure 8**

8. Sew the center row between the top and bottom rows to complete the Dust Storm A block as shown in Figure 8; press seams open.

9. To complete a Dust Storm B block, sew a K-M-N unit between two brown A-B units to make the center row as shown in Figure 9; press seams open.

Figure 9

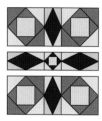

Figure 10

10. Join two L corner units with a brown A-B unit to make the top row as shown in Figure 10; press seams open. Repeat to make the bottom row.

11. Sew the center row between the top and bottom rows to complete one Dust Storm B block as shown in Figure 11; press seams open.

Figure 11

12. Repeat steps 9–11 to complete a second Dust Storm B block.

Completing the Top

1. Sew O to each side of P to make an O-P unit as shown in Figure 12; press seams toward O. Repeat to make 10 O-P units.

Figure 12   **Figure 13**

2. Sew two each peach/tan B and BR pieces to a gray tonal A as shown in Figure 13; press seams away from A. Repeat to make 20 gray A-B units.

3. Sew Q to each side of C; press seams toward C.

4. Sew O to each side of the C-Q unit to complete a C-Q-O unit as shown in Figure 14; press seams toward O. Repeat to make eight C-Q-O units.

Figure 14   **Figure 15**

5. Sew an O-P unit between two gray A-B units to make an A-B-O-P strip as shown in Figure 15; press seams open. Repeat to make 10 A-B-O-P strips.

6. Sew an A-B-O-P strip to the top and bottom of each pieced block; press seams open.

7. Sew a C-Q-O unit to each end of the remaining A-B-O-P strips to make four sashing strips as shown in Figure 16; press seams open.

Figure 16

8. Join the bordered blocks with the sashing strips to complete the pieced center; press seams open.

9. Join the R strips on short ends to make one long strip; press seams open. Subcut strip into two 70" R strips.

10. Repeat step 9 with T strips to cut two 73" T strips.

11. Repeat step 9 with V strips to cut two 78" V strips.

12. Sew an R strip to opposite long sides and S strips to the short ends of the pieced center; press seams toward R and S strips.

13. Sew a T strip to opposite long sides and U strips to the short ends of the pieced center; press seams toward T and U strips.

14. Sew the V strips to opposite long sides and W strips to the short ends of the pieced center; press seams toward V and W strips to complete the pieced top.

15. Layer, quilt and bind referring to Finishing Your Quilt on page 173. ✤

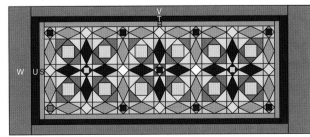

Dust Storm Bed Warmer
Placement Diagram 91" x 37½"

A
Cut 12 dark brown tonal & 20 gray tonal

B
Cut 104 peach/tan print & 24 cream tonal (reverse half of each for BR)

Diamond Flush

The on-point setting of the blocks and fabric choices of batiks, brown and tan give this bed warmer a masculine touch.

Design by **JULIE WEAVER**

PROJECT NOTE

Feminize this bed warmer by using pretty florals and pastels. A floral print with large motifs could be centered in the A squares or an appliquéd floral motif could be added to make this a pleasing project for women.

PROJECT SPECIFICATIONS

Skill Level: Beginner
Quilt Size: 74½" x 36½"
Block Size: 10" x 10"
Number of Blocks: 4

MATERIALS

- ⅓ yard total assorted batiks
- 1½ yards tan mottled
- 2¼ yards brown tonal print
- Batting 80" x 42"
- Backing 80" x 42"
- Neutral-color all-purpose thread
- Quilting thread
- Basic sewing tools and supplies

Cutting

1. Cut one 6½" by fabric width strip tan mottled; subcut strip into four 6½" A squares.

2. Cut one 2½" by fabric width strip tan mottled; subcut strip into eight 2½" D squares.

3. Cut two 2⅞" by fabric width strips tan mottled; subcut strips into (28) 2⅞" squares B squares.

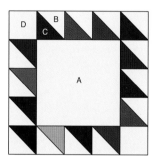

Diamond Flush
10" x 10" Block
Make 4

4. Cut one 15½" by fabric width strip tan mottled; subcut strip into two 15½" squares. Cut each square on both diagonals to make eight H triangles; discard two.

5. Cut one 8" by fabric width strip tan mottled; subcut strip into two 8" squares. Cut each square in half on one diagonal to make four I triangles.

6. Cut four 2" by fabric width K strips tan mottled.

7. Cut 28 total 2⅞" x 2⅞" C squares assorted batiks.

8. Cut three 1½" x 1½" F squares and five 1⅞" x 1⅞" squares assorted batiks; cut the 1⅞" x 1⅞" squares in half on one diagonal to make (10) G triangles.

9. Cut four 1½" by fabric width strips brown tonal print; subcut strips into (16) 10½" E strips.

10. Cut four 3½" by fabric width J strips brown tonal print.

11. Cut four 6½" by fabric width L strips brown tonal print.

12. Cut two 6½" x 37" M strips brown tonal print.

13. Cut six 2¼" by fabric width strips brown tonal print for binding.

Completing the Blocks

Note: *Use a ¼" seam allowance throughout.*

1. Draw a diagonal line from corner to corner on the wrong side of each B square.

2. Place a B square right sides together with C; stitch ¼" on each side of the marked line as shown in Figure 1.

Figure 1

3. Cut the stitched unit on the marked line to complete two B-C units, again referring to Figure 1; press seams toward C.

4. Repeat steps 2 and 3 with all B and C squares to complete 56 B-C units.

5. To complete one Diamond Flush block, join three B-C units to make a B-C row as shown in Figure 2; press seams in one direction. Repeat to make two B-C rows.

Figure 2

6. Sew a B-C row to opposite sides of A as shown in Figure 3; press seams toward A.

Figure 3

7. Join four B-C units with a D square to make a B-C-D row as shown in Figure 4; press seams toward D. Repeat to make two B-C-D rows.

Figure 4

8. Sew a B-C-D row to the remaining sides of A referring to Figure 5 to complete one Diamond Flush block; press seams toward A.

Figure 5

9. Repeat steps 5–8 to complete four Diamond Flush blocks.

Completing the Top

1. Sew an E strip to opposite sides of each Diamond Flush block; press seams toward E strips.

2. Sew H pieces to an E/block to make a diagonal row as shown in Figure 6; press seams toward E strips. Repeat to make two diagonal rows.

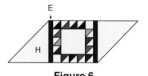

Figure 6

3. Join two E strips with F and add G to each end to make an E-F-G strip as shown in Figure 7; press seams toward E. Repeat to make three E-F-G strips.

Figure 7

4. Join the two diagonal rows with the three E-F-G strips to make a block section as shown in Figure 8; press seams toward the E-F-G strips.

Figure 8

5. Sew G to each end of each remaining E strip to make an E-G strip as shown in Figure 9; press seams toward E strip. Repeat to make two E-G strips.

Figure 9

6. Sew an E-G strip to one side of each remaining block as shown in Figure 10; press seams toward E-G strips.

Figure 10

7. Sew H and I pieces to each E-G/block to make end sections as shown in Figure 11; press seams toward H and I pieces.

Figure 11

8. Sew the end sections to the block section to complete the pieced center referring to the Placement Diagram for positioning of sections; press seams toward end sections.

9. Join the J strips on short ends to make one long strip; press seams open. Repeat with K and L strips.

10. Sew the K strip between the J and L strips along length to make a long strip set; press seams in one direction.

11. Subcut the J-K-L strip set into two 63" border strips.

12. Sew a border strip to opposite long sides of the pieced center; press seams toward the border strips.

13. Sew an M strip to each end to complete the pieced top; press seams toward M strips.

14. Layer, quilt and bind referring to Finishing Your Quilt on page 173. ✤

Diamond Flush
Placement Diagram 74½" x 36½"

Tip **Joining strips on short ends with diagonal seams helps keep the seam from being so obvious and when used for binding, it results in less bulk all in one place.** To make a diagonal seam place one strip perpendicular to and right sides together with another strip as shown in Figure 12; draw a diagonal line from the inside corner to the outside corner of the top strip, again referring to Figure 12. Stitch on the marked line, trim the seam to ¼" and press open to complete the seam.

Figure 12

Summer Trellis

Make an elegant bed warmer with an oriental flair using sashiko stitching.

Design by SUSAN FLETCHER

PROJECT SPECIFICATIONS

It is best to pre-wash your fabric and batting before using; press fabric to remove all wrinkles.

PROJECT SPECIFICATIONS

Skill Level: Intermediate
Quilt Size: 84½" x 20½"

MATERIALS

- ¼ yard navy/pink floral
- 2½ yards navy blue solid
- Batting 85½" x 21"
- Navy blue all-purpose thread
- Sashiko thread or white pearl cotton
- Sashiko needle or embroidery needle size 7 or 8
- Fine-tip permanent ink fabric marker
- 2½" yards at least 22"-wide white fusible, non-woven, lightweight interfacing
- Basic sewing tools and supplies

Cutting

1. Prepare template for circle pattern; cut as directed.

2. Cut one 86½" x 21" rectangle navy blue solid for top and one 85" x 21" rectangle for backing.

3. Cut one fusible interfacing piece 86½" x 21".

Completing the Top

1. Using pattern given, prepare circle designs for appliqué by machine-stitching ⅜" from the edge all around.

2. Make several copies of the sashiko stitching design given. Tape the copies end to end to make the pattern approximately 84" with 30 short bars in the design.

3. Lay the fusible side of the interfacing on the prepared pattern 1¼" from each end and 3¼" in from side edge as shown in Figure 1; trace the sashiko grid design onto the interfacing.

4. Starting 3¼" from the opposite side, trace the design a second time, again referring to Figure 1.

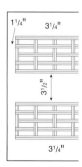

Figure 1

5. Decide on the stitched flower placement and trace the design on the grid as desired. Mark the placement of the finished size of the circles onto the marked sashiko design as desired and referring to the Placement Diagram for positioning suggestion. ***Note:*** *If the circles and flowers over the other marked lines are too confusing for you, use a different color permanent fabric marker to trace circles and flowers.*

6. Fuse the marked fusible interfacing to the wrong side of the prepared top beginning in the

center and working toward the edges, lifting and setting your iron down, rather than sliding it to prevent distortion.

Sashiko Stitching

1. To stitch sashiko, which translates literally to mean "little stabs," use a simple running stitch. *Note: You are going to stitch this project from the back (interfacing) side. Make the stitches on the interfacing side shorter than those that will show on the fabric side. Begin and end all stitching on the interfacing side.*

2. To stitch, begin with a comfortable length of white thread about 24"–30" long without a knot.

3. Refer to Figure 2 to begin stitching; insert the needle through the interfacing to the fabric side on a design line, leaving a 1" tail on the interfacing side. Move the needle ¼" along the design and bring it back to the interfacing side. Move ⅛" along the design and go through to the fabric side. Come back up ¼" along the line; make one more stitch. Slide the needle through the previous stitches on the interfacing side and then back down to the fabric side ⅛" from the starting point. Pull stitches tight to secure thread end, but do not gather.

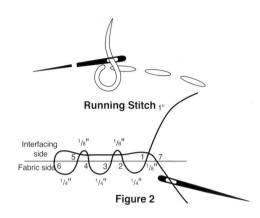

Running Stitch

Figure 2

4. Continue stitching using a running stitch until you are near the end of the thread, then pass the needle under a few stitches on the interfacing side to secure the thread end.

5. For subsequent threads, begin by passing the needle under two or three stitches on the interfacing side.

6. Stitch along all marked lines including the circles and flowers.

Completing the Top

1. Place a fabric circle inside each of the stitched circles on the top; turn the raw edges of the fabric circle under along the stitched line with the needle as you blindstitch the circle in place.

2. Trim the top ¾" beyond each end of the stitched design to complete the top.

Completing the Bed Warmer

1. Place the batting on a flat surface; place the stitched top right side up on the batting.

2. Place the backing piece right sides together with the layered batting and top; stitch all around using a ¼" seam allowance and leaving a 6" opening on one side.

3. Clip corners; turn right side out through opening. Press edges flat at seam.

4. Turn opening edges to the inside ¼" and hand-stitch opening closed to finish. ✤

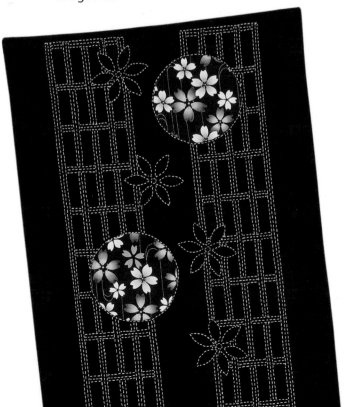

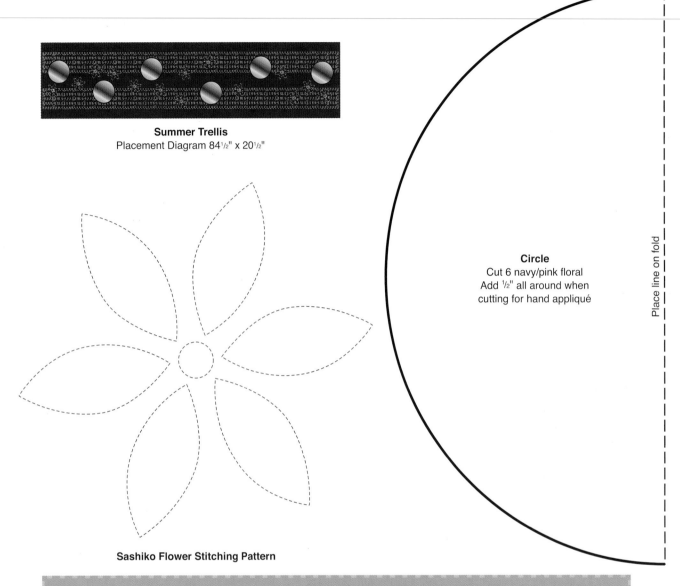

Summer Trellis
Placement Diagram 84½" x 20½"

Circle
Cut 6 navy/pink floral
Add ½" all around when
cutting for hand appliqué

Place line on fold

Sashiko Flower Stitching Pattern

Sashiko Tips

Sashiko stitches will be smoother and faster if you use your left hand to feed the fabric onto the needle while holding the needle steady with your right hand.

Put as many stitches on the needle as you find comfortable before pulling the needle through. With practice it is possible to put about 3" on the needle at one time.

Do not use a hoop when stitching; instead gather the fabric in your hand, sit in a comfortable chair and relax while you stitch.

Avoid pulling the thread snug or the cloth will pucker. Check for this frequently at first. Leaving a little slack in the thread on the back whenever you turn a corner or cross from one line of stitching to a new line will help to avoid this.

Experiment with stitch length and thread weight. A rule of thumb for stitch length is 4–8 stitches per inch, with the stitches on the top of the fabric being two or three times the length of the stitches on the back. You will find your own rhythm quite quickly

Sashiko Trellis Stitching Pattern

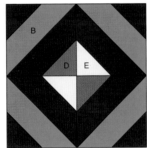

Foot-of-the-Bed Warmer

Keep toasty warm with a patchwork bed comforter.

Design by JILL REBER

PROJECT SPECIFICATIONS

Skill Level: Beginner
Quilt Size: 82" x 22"
Block Size: 10" x 10"
Number of Blocks: 7

Reflecting Pool
10" x 10" Block
Make 7

MATERIALS

- ⅛ yard light gold tonal
- ⅛ yard dark gold tonal
- ⅝ yard rust tonal
- ⅞ yard green tonal
- 1⅛ yards brown print
- Batting 88" x 28"
- Backing 88" x 28"
- Neutral-color all-purpose thread
- Quilting thread
- Basic sewing tools and supplies

Cutting

1. Cut two 5⅞" by fabric width strips rust tonal; subcut strips into (14) 5⅞" squares. Cut each square in half on one diagonal to make 28 A triangles.

2. Cut two 3" by fabric width strips rust tonal; subcut strips into (28) 3" C squares.

3. Cut two 5⅞" by fabric width strips green tonal; subcut strips into (14) 5⅞" squares. Cut each square in half on one diagonal to make 28 B triangles.

4. Cut one 2½" by fabric width strip green tonal; subcut strip into two 10½" F strips.

5. Cut four 2½" by fabric width G strips green tonal.

6. Cut one 3" by fabric width strip dark gold tonal; subcut strip into (14) 3" D squares.

7. Cut one 3" by fabric width strip light gold tonal; subcut strip into (14) 3" E squares.

8. Cut one 4½" by fabric width strip brown print; subcut strip into two 14½" H strips.

9. Cut four 4½" by fabric width I strips brown print.

10. Cut six 2¼" by fabric width brown print for binding.

Completing the Blocks

Note: *Use a ¼" seam allowance throughout.*

1. To complete one Reflecting Pool block, sew an A triangle to a B triangle along the diagonal to make an A-B unit as shown in Figure 1; press seam toward A. Repeat to make four A-B units.

Figure 1

2. Mark a diagonal line from corner to corner on all C, D and E squares.

3. Place a D square on the A corner of one A-B unit and stitch on the marked line as shown in Figure 2; trim seam to ¼" and press D to the right side, again referring to Figure 2.

Figure 2

4. Repeat step 3 with C on the B side of the A-B-D unit as shown in Figure 3 to complete a block quarter; repeat to complete two D block quarters.

Figure 3

5. Repeat steps 3 and 4 using A, B, C and E to complete two E block quarters as shown in Figure 4.

Figure 4

6. Join one each D and E block quarters to make a row as shown in Figure 5; press seam toward the D block quarter. Repeat to make two rows.

Figure 5

7. Join the two rows to complete one block referring to the block drawing; press seam in one direction.

8. Repeat Steps 1 and 3–7 to complete seven Reflecting Pool blocks.

Completing the Top

1. Join the blocks to complete the pieced center; press seams in one direction.

2. Sew an F strip to each short end of the pieced center; press seams toward F strips.

3. Join the G strips on short ends to make one long strip; press seams open. Subcut strip into two 74½" G strips.

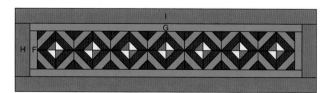

Foot of the Bed Warmer
Placement Diagram 82" x 22"

4. Sew a G strip to opposite long sides of the pieced center; press seams toward G strips.

5. Sew an H strip to short ends of the pieced center; press seams toward H strips.

6. Join the I strips on short ends to make one long strip; press seams open. Subcut strip into two 82½" I strips.

7. Sew an I strip to opposite long sides of the pieced center; press seams toward I strips to complete the pieced top.

8. Layer, quilt and bind referring to Finishing Your Quilt on page 173. ❖

Scrappy Confusion

Matching pillow shams really highlight a bed warmer.

Design by CONNIE KAUFFMAN

PROJECT NOTES

Materials listed and instructions given make one bed warmer and two pillow shams.

PROJECT SPECIFICATIONS

Skill Level: Intermediate
Bed Warmer Size: 75" x 35"
Pillow Sham Size: 35" x 25"
Block Size: 10" x 10"
Number of Blocks: 24

MATERIALS

- ⅝ yard dark print
- 1 yard total tan scraps
- 1½ yards total white tonal scraps
- 1⅝ yards fabric for pillow-sham backs
- 2⅜ yards total dark scraps
- Batting 81" x 41" and (2) 41" x 31"
- Backing 81" x 41" and (2) 41" x 31"
- Neutral-color all-purpose thread
- Quilting thread
- Basic sewing tools and supplies

Cutting

1. Cut (36) 2⅞" x 7⅝" strips each white tonal scraps (A) and dark scraps (B).

2. Cut (24) 5⅞" x 5⅞" squares each tan scraps (C) and dark scraps (D). Cut each square in half on one diagonal to make 48 each C and D triangles.

3. Cut 3" x 10½" strips as follows: 26 white tonal scraps (E), 34 dark scraps (F) and eight tan scraps (G).

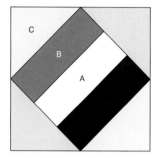

Light Confusion
10" x 10" Block
Make 12

Dark Confusion
10" x 10" Block
Make 12

4. Cut 24 total 3" x 3" I squares white tonal and tan scraps.

5. Cut 20 total 3" x 3" H squares dark scraps.

6. Cut four 25½" x 21" backing fabric pieces for pillow shams.

7. Cut six 2¼" by fabric width strips dark print for binding.

Completing the Blocks

Note: *Use a ¼" seam allowance throughout.*

1. To complete one Light Confusion block, join two B strips and one A strip as shown in Figure 1; press seams toward B strips.

Figure 1

2. Sew a C triangle to each side of the A-B unit to complete one Light Confusion block; press seams toward A-B.

3. Repeat steps 1 and 2 to complete 12 Light Confusion blocks.

4. To complete one Dark Confusion block, join two A strips and one B strip as shown in Figure 2; press seams toward B strips.

Figure 2

5. Sew a D triangle to each side of the A-B unit to complete one Dark Confusion block; press seams toward D.

6. Repeat steps 4 and 5 to complete 12 Dark Confusion blocks.

Completing the Bed Warmer Top

1. Join two E and one F strips to make an E-F unit as shown in Figure 3; press seams toward E. Repeat to make eight E-F units.

Figure 3

2. Join two F and one G strips to make an F-G unit as shown in Figure 4; press seams toward G. Repeat to make eight F-G units.

Figure 4

3. Sew an H square between two I squares to make a light row as shown in Figure 5; press seams toward H. Repeat to make eight light rows.

Figure 5

4. Sew an I square between two H squares to make a dark row as shown in Figure 6; press seams toward H. Repeat to make four dark rows.

Figure 6

5. Sew a dark row between two light rows to make a corner unit as shown in Figure 7; press seams in one direction. Repeat to make four corner units.

Figure 7

6. Join three E-F and three F-G units to make a side row referring to Figure 8;

press seams in one direction. Repeat to make two side rows.

Figure 8

7. Sew a side row to opposite long sides of the pieced center; press seams toward the side rows.

8. Join one each E-F and F-G units with a corner unit on each end referring to Figure 9 to make an end row; press seams away from corner units. Repeat to make two end rows.

Figure 9

9. Sew an end row on opposite ends of the pieced center to complete the bed-warmer top; press seams toward end rows.

10. Layer, quilt and bind referring to Finishing Your Quilt on page 173.

Completing the Pillow Sham Tops

1. To complete one pillow-sham top, sew one Light Confusion block between two Dark Confusion blocks to make a row as shown in Figure 10; press seams in one direction.

Figure 10

2. Sew one Dark Confusion block between two Light Confusion blocks to make a row, again referring to Figure 10; press seams in one direction.

3. Join the two rows with seams in opposite directions, again referring to Figure 10; press seam in one direction.

4. Join one E strip with two F strips on short ends to make an F-E-F strip as shown in Figure 11; press seams toward F.

5. Repeat step 4 with one F strip and two E strips to make an E-F-E strip, again referring to Figure 11.

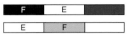

Figure 11

6. Sew an E-F-E strip to the long side with two dark blocks and the F-E-F strip to the remaining long side; press seams toward strips.

7. Join one each E and F strips on short ends to make an E-F strip; press seam toward F. Repeat to make two E-F strips.

8. Sew an H square to the E end and an I square to the F end of each strip to complete two end strips referring to Figure 12.

Figure 12

9. Sew an end strip to opposite ends of the pieced center to complete one pillow sham top; press seams toward end strips.

10. Repeat steps 1–9 to complete two pillow sham tops.

Completing the Pillow Shams

1. Sandwich one pillow-sham batting piece between the pieced top and one prepared pillow-sham backing piece.

2. Quilt as desired by hand or machine; when quilting is complete trim edges even.

3. Turn under ¼" on one 25½" edge of each 25½" x 21" backing rectangle and press. Turn under another ¼", press and stitch to hem each rectangle.

4. Lay one quilted pillow-sham top right side up on a flat surface; lay one hemmed backing rectangle right sides together with the quilted pillow sham matching raw edges.

5. Lay a second backing rectangle on the opposite end of the quilted pillow sham as in step 4, overlapping hemmed edges as shown in Figure 13.

Figure 13

6. Stitch all around; trim corners and turn right side out.

7. Press edges flat; stitch in the ditch along the inner border seam.

8. Insert pillow through back opening to use.

9. Repeat steps 4–8 to complete the second pillow sham. ❖

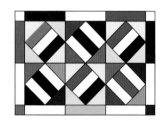

Scrappy Confusion Pillow Sham
Placement Diagram 35" x 25"

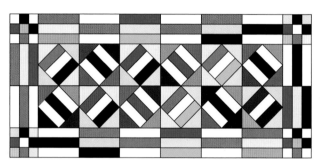

Scrappy Confusion Bed Warmer
Placement Diagram 75" x 35"

Rolls & Squares

Whether you buy the convenient precuts available today, or cut them yourself, using rolls of 2½-inch strips, 1½-inch strips and squares that are 5 or 10 inches, makes it easier and faster to complete your quilt. These are great patterns for beginners or those short on time.

Hopscotch

Only two blocks are used in this random-looking quilt.

Design by **LYNN SCHIEFELBEIN**

PROJECT NOTES

Press all fabrics before you cut; use steam and fabric finish or starch. The steam helps to preshrink the fabric. After pressing, hold the selvage edges together and slide back and forth until it hangs perfectly straight without ripples. Lay it down and carefully match the folded edge with the selvage edge to make a four-layer piece. This will help you cut even, straight strips with no wavy edges. If using spray starch, you will need to wash your quilt upon completion. Insects love to munch on spray starch. Most fabric-finish sprays do not contain starch so there is usually no need to wash after you finish. Read the product label to be sure.

PROJECT SPECIFICATIONS

Skill Level: Intermediate
Quilt Size: 54½" x 61"
Block Size: 13" x 6½"
Number of Blocks: 21

MATERIALS

- 1 Jelly Roll™ or (40) 2½" x 42" hand-dyed strips
- 42 (5") hand-dyed squares in a variety of colors for A pieces
- ⅜ yard lime-green hand-dyed
- ½ yard orange hand-dyed
- 1½ yards magenta hand-dyed
- Batting 61" x 67"
- Backing 61" x 67"
- Neutral-color all-purpose thread
- Quilting thread
- Fabric-finish spray or spray starch optional
- Basic sewing tools and supplies

Hopscotch A
13" x 6½" Block
Make 12

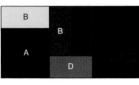

Hopscotch B
13" x 6½" Block
Make 9

Cutting

1. Cut strips from Jelly Roll or 2½" x 42" hand-dyed strips as follows: (24) 7" C strips, (60) 5" B strips and nine 4½" D strips.

2. Cut five 2½" by fabric width E/F strips orange hand-dyed.

3. Cut five 1¾" by fabric width G/H strips lime-green hand-dyed.

4. Cut six 5" by fabric width I/J strips magenta hand-dyed.

5. Cut seven 2¼" by fabric width strips magenta hand-dyed for binding.

Completing the Hopscotch A Blocks

Note: *Use a ¼" seam allowance throughout.*

1. To complete one Hopscotch A block, sew A to B; press seam toward B. Repeat to make two A-B units.

2. Add C to the left side edge of each A-B unit as shown in Figure 1; press seam toward C.

Figure 1

3. Join the two A-B-C units as shown in Figure 2 to complete one Hopscotch A block; press seam to the right.

Figure 2

4. Repeat steps 1–3 to complete 12 Hopscotch A blocks, pressing seams to the right on half the blocks and to the left on the remaining blocks.

Completing the Hopscotch B Blocks

1. Join two B pieces; press seam in one direction.

2. Add D to the bottom of the B unit as shown in Figure 3; press seam toward B.

Figure 3   **Figure 4**

3. Sew B to A; press seam toward B. Repeat to make two A-B units.

4. Sew the B-D unit between the two A-B units to complete one Hopscotch B block as shown in Figure 4; press seams in one direction.

5. Repeat steps 1–4 to complete nine Hopscotch B blocks.

Completing the Top

1. Join three A blocks with seams pointing toward the right to make an X row as shown in Figure 5; press joining seams toward the left. Repeat to make four X rows.

Figure 5   **Figure 6**

2. Join three B blocks with seams pointing toward the left to make a Y row as shown in Figure 6; press joining seams toward the right. Repeat to make three Y rows.

3. Join the X and Y rows, alternating placement, referring to the Placement Diagram for positioning; press seams in one direction to complete the pieced center.

4. Join the E/F strips on short ends to make one long strip; press seams open. Subcut strip into two 46" E strips and two 43½" F strips.

5. Sew an E strip to opposite long sides and F strips to the top and bottom of the pieced center; press seams toward E and F strips.

6. Repeat step 4 to cut two 50" G strips and two 46" H strips.

7. Repeat step 5, sewing G to the long sides and H to the top and bottom.

8. Repeat step 4 to cut two 52½" I strips and two 55" J strips.

9. Repeat step 5, sewing I to the long sides and J to the top and bottom to complete the top.

10. Layer, quilt and bind referring to Finishing Your Quilt on page 173. ❖

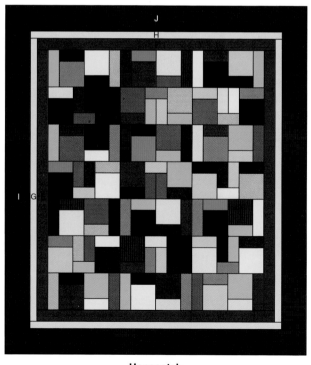

Hopscotch
Placement Diagram 54½" x 61"

Plum Jelly Stars

Use up leftover Jelly Roll™ strips or cut your own to make this fabulous baby quilt or wall hanging.

Design by JULIE HIGGINS

PROJECT SPECIFICATIONS

Skill Level: Advanced
Quilt Size: 44" x 44"
Block Size: 15" x 15"
Number of Blocks: 4

MATERIALS

- 5 brown Jelly Roll strips or cut (5) 2½" x 42" strips
- 4 each peach, gold and lavender Jelly Roll strips or cut 4 each 2½" x 42"
- ⅝ yard cream print
- ¾ yard cream/peach/lavender print
- 1 yard lavender dot
- Batting 50" x 50"
- Backing 50" x 50"
- Neutral-color all-purpose thread
- Quilting thread
- Spray starch
- Basic sewing tools and supplies

Cutting

1. Cut four 2½" x 30½" D strips lavender dot.

2. Cut one 5½" by fabric width strip lavender dot; subcut strip into four 5½" G squares.

3. Cut five 2¼" by fabric width strips lavender dot for binding.

4. Cut four 2½" x 2½" E squares from one brown Jelly Roll strip.

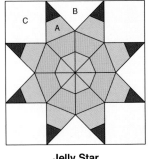

Jelly Star
15" x 15" Block
Make 4

5. Cut four 5½" x 34½" F strips cream/peach/lavender print.

6. Cut two 4⅞" by fabric width strips cream print; subcut strips into (16) 4⅞" C squares.

7. Cut one 7½" by fabric width strip cream print; subcut strips into four 7½" squares. Cut each square on both diagonals to make 16 B triangles.

Completing the Blocks

Note: Use a ¼" seam allowance throughout.

1. Select one each brown, peach, gold and lavender Jelly Roll or 2½" x 42" strips; join with right sides together along length to make a strip set; press seams open. Repeat to make four strip sets. *Note: Because the edges of the A shapes will be bias, it helps to starch the strip sets.*

2. Prepare template for A using pattern given.

3. Place the A template on one strip set as shown in Figure 1; cut out eight A pieces from the strip set, marking dots from template on A pieces. Repeat with each strip set.

Figure 1

4. To complete one Jelly Star block, select a set of eight matching A pieces; join two pieces stopping stitching at dots at the end of the seams as shown in Figure 2; press seam in one direction. Repeat to make four two-unit sections.

Figure 2   **Figure 3**

5. Join two two-unit sections to make half the star as in step 4 and referring to Figure 3; press seam in one direction. Repeat to make two halves.

6. Join the two halves, matching seams to complete the pieced star shape; press seam in the same direction as before.

7. Sew in B pieces at sides, stitching from the center to the outside edge on each side as shown in Figure 4; press seam away from D.

Figure 4

8. Sew in C pieces at the corners as in step 7 to complete one Jelly Star block; press seams toward C.

9. Repeat steps 4–8 to complete four Jelly Star blocks.

Completing the Top

1. Join two Jelly Star blocks to make a row; press seam in one direction. Repeat to make two rows.

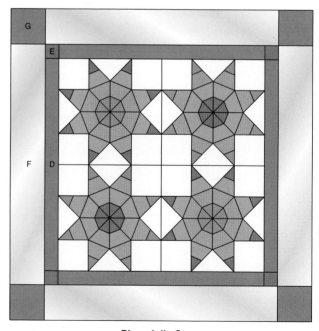

Plum Jelly Stars
Placement Diagram 44" x 44"

2. Join the rows with seams going in opposite directions to complete the pieced center; press seam in one direction.

3. Sew a D strip to opposite sides of the pieced center; press seams toward the D strips.

4. Sew E to each end of each remaining D strip; press seams toward E.

5. Sew a D-E strip to the remaining sides of the pieced center; press seams toward the D-E strips.

6. Sew F to opposite sides of the pieced center; press seams toward F.

7. Sew G to each end of each remaining F strip; press seams toward F.

8. Sew an F-G strip to the remaining sides of the pieced center; press seams toward F-G strips to complete the pieced top.

9. Layer, quilt and bind referring to Finishing Your Quilt on page 173. ❖

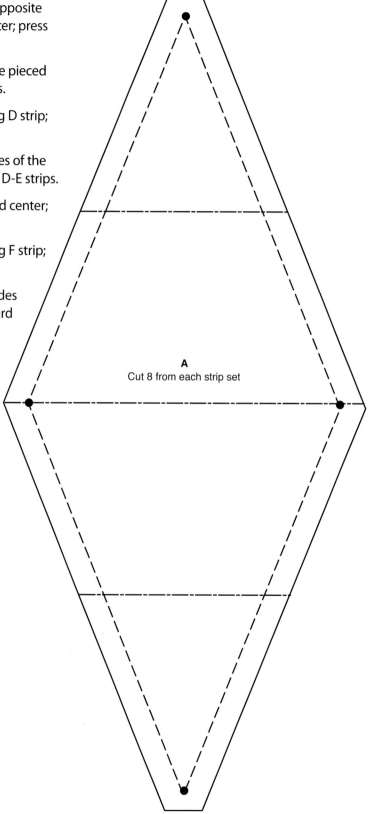

A
Cut 8 from each strip set

Purple Pandemonium

Sew up this quilt using charm squares and fat quarters.

Design by **KONDA LUCKAU**

PROJECT SPECIFICATIONS

Skill Level: Beginner
Quilt Size: 48" x 60"
Block Size: 12" x 12"
Number of Blocks: 20

MATERIALS

- 40 (5") B charm squares from the purple family
- 10 fat quarters from the purple family
- ⅝ yard purple mottled
- Batting 54" x 66"
- Backing 54" x 66"
- Neutral-color all-purpose thread
- Quilting thread
- Basic sewing tools and supplies

Cutting

1. Cut each fat quarter into two 2" x 9½" A strips, two 6½" x 9½" C rectangles and two 3½" x 12½" D strips as shown in Figure 1 for layout.

Figure 1

2. Cut six 2¼" by fabric width strips purple mottled for binding.

Completing the Blocks

Note: *Use a ¼" seam allowance throughout.*

1. Randomly select two B squares; join. Press seam in one direction. Repeat for 20 B units.

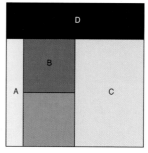

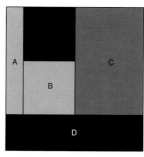

Purple Pandemonium A
12" x 12" Block
Make 10

Purple Pandemonium B
12" x 12" Block
Make 10

2. Sew an A strip to the left side and a C rectangle to the right side of each of the B units as shown in Figure 2; press seams toward A and C.

Figure 2

3. Randomly separate the 20 partial blocks into two sets of 10.

4. Sew a D strip to the top edge of each partial block in one set to complete 10 A blocks referring to Figure 3; press seams toward D.

Figure 3

5. Sew D to the bottom of each partial block in the remaining set to complete 10 B blocks referring to Figure 4; press seams toward D.

Figure 4

Completing the Top

1. Join two each Purple Pandemonium A and B blocks to make an X row beginning with an A block as shown in Figure 5; press seams toward A blocks. Repeat to make three X rows.

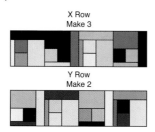

X Row
Make 3

Y Row
Make 2

Figure 5

2. Repeat step 1 to make two Y rows, beginning each row with a B block, again referring to Figure 5; press seam toward the A blocks.

3. Join the rows beginning and ending with X rows referring to the Placement Diagram for positioning; press seams in one direction.

4. Layer, quilt and bind referring to Finishing Your Quilt on page 173. ❖

Purple Pandemonium
Placement Diagram 48" x 60"

Flirty Thirties

Use charms and strips, and finish this pretty quilt in a weekend.

Design by **KAREN BLOCHER**

PROJECT SPECIFICATIONS

Skill Level: Intermediate
Quilt Size: 48" x 48"
Block Size: 5⅞" x 5⅞"
Number of Blocks: 16

MATERIALS

- 16 (5" x 5") 1930s reproduction print charm squares
- 1 Jelly Roll™ or 12 (2½" x 42") strips 1930s reproduction prints
- 4 (6½" x 6½") I squares 1930s reproduction prints
- ⅜ yard white solid
- ¾ yard blue/white mini-check
- ⅞ yard gold print
- Batting 54" x 54"
- Backing 54" x 54"
- Neutral-color all-purpose thread
- Quilting thread
- Spray starch
- Basic sewing tools and supplies

Cutting

1. Cut each 5" x 5" square in half on one diagonal to make 32 A triangles.

2. Cut two 5" by fabric width strips white solid; subcut strips into (16) 5" squares. Cut each square in half on one diagonal to make (32) B triangles.

3. Cut two 6⅜" by fabric width strips blue/white mini-check; subcut strips into nine 6⅜" C squares.

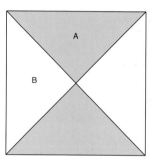

Triangles
5⅞" x 5⅞" Block
Make 16

4. Cut one 9½" by fabric width strip blue/white mini-check; subcut strip into three 9½" squares and two 5" x 5" squares. Cut each 9½" x 9½" square on both diagonals to make 12 D triangles. Cut each 5" x 5" square in half on one diagonal to make four E triangles.

5. Cut two 1¾" x 34" F strips and two 1¾" x 36½" G strips gold print.

6. Cut (72) 6½" H strips from the 2½" x 42" strips.

7. Cut a total of (250") 2½"-wide bias strips gold print for binding. ***Note:*** *Use bias binding on curves because it stretches around the curved areas.*

Completing the Blocks

Note: *Use a ¼" seam allowance throughout.*

1. Apply spray starch to the long bias edge of each A and B triangle to prevent stretching.

2. To complete one Triangles block, select two matching A triangles. Sew an A triangle to a

B triangle as shown in Figure 1; press seam toward A. Repeat to make two A-B units.

Figure 1

3. Join two A-B units to complete one Triangles block referring to Figure 2; press seam in one direction.

Figure 2

4. Repeat steps 2 and 3 to complete 16 Triangles blocks.

Completing the Top

1. Arrange blocks with C squares and D and E triangles to make diagonal rows referring to Figure 3; join as arranged to make rows. Press seams away from the Triangles blocks.

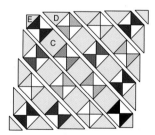

Figure 3

2. Join the rows as arranged to complete the pieced center; press seams in one direction.

3. Sew an F strip to the top and bottom and G strips to opposite sides of the pieced center; press seams toward F and G strips.

4. Join 18 H pieces on the long sides to complete a side strip; press seams in one direction. Repeat to make four side strips.

5. Sew a side strip to opposite sides of the pieced center; press seams toward G strips.

6. Sew an I square to both ends of each remaining side strip; press seams toward I.

7. Sew the I/side strips to the top and bottom of the pieced center; press seams toward F strips.

8. Using the pattern given, mark the scallop shape on each side of the pieced top, starting in the center of each side by aligning the center mark on the pattern with the center seam on each side and working toward the corners as shown in Figure 4.

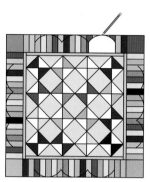

Figure 4

9. Use a large dinner plate or pizza pan to mark corner curve, connecting the corner curve to the ends of the curves on the sides as shown in Figure 5.

Figure 5

10. Trim on the marked lines to complete the pieced top.

11. Layer, quilt and bind referring to Finishing Your Quilt on page 173. ✤

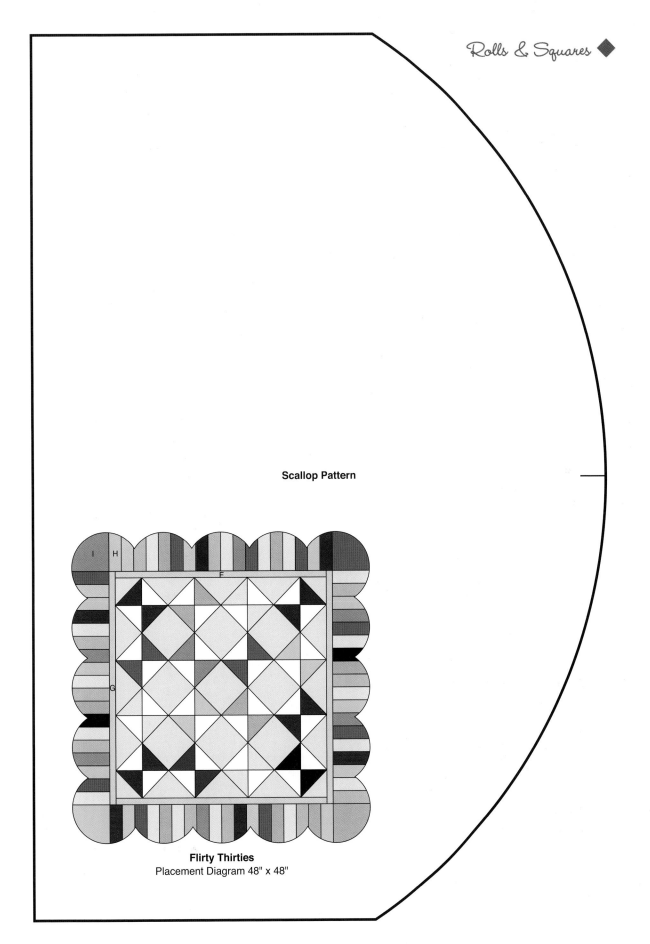

Scallop Pattern

Flirty Thirties
Placement Diagram 48" x 48"

The bright colors of spring make this a perfect quilt for a daily pick-me-up.

Design by **CONNIE KAUFFMAN**

PROJECT SPECIFICATIONS

Skill Level: Intermediate
Quilt Size: 53½" x 67"
Block Size: 4½" x 4½"
Number of Blocks: 24

MATERIALS

- 61 spring-color charm squares for A (5" x 5" squares)
- ⅝ yard floral print
- ⅔ yard light orange print
- ⅞ yard white tonal
- 1⅓ yards green print
- Batting 60" x 73"
- Backing 60" x 73"
- All-purpose thread to match fabrics
- Quilting thread
- Basic sewing tools and supplies

Cutting

1. Select 24 A charm squares and trim to 3¾" x 3¾" squares for piece 1.

2. Cut three 5" by fabric width strips white tonal; subcut strips into (17) 5" B squares. Trim the one remaining strip to 3¼"; subcut strip into (11) 3¼" squares for pieces 2–5.

3. Cut three 3¼" by fabric width strips white tonal; subcut strips into (37) 3¼" squares to total 48 squares. Cut each square in half on one diagonal to make 96 triangles for pieces 2–5.

Square-in-a-Square
4½" x 4½" Block
Make 24

4. Cut two 5" x 32" D strips and two 5" x 36½" C strips light orange print.

5. Cut six 7" by fabric width E/F strips green print.

6. Cut six 2¼" by fabric width strips floral print for binding.

Completing the Blocks

1. Make 24 copies of the paper-piecing pattern given.

2. Set machine stitch length to 15 stitches per inch or 1.5.

3. Pin one A square right side up in the number 1 position on the unmarked side of the paper.

4. Place piece 2 right sides together with piece 1; stitch on the 1–2 line on the marked side

of the paper as shown in Figure 1. Press piece 2 to the right side.

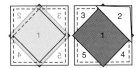

Figure 1

5. Repeat step 4 with pieces 3–5 to complete one Square-in-a-Square block; press all pieces to the right side after stitching.

6. Trim the pieced block to 5" x 5"; remove paper foundation.

7. Repeat steps 3–6 to complete 24 Square-in-a-Square blocks.

8. Return machine stitch length to normal size.

Completing the Top

1. Join two Square-in-a-Square blocks with three A squares to make an X row as shown in Figure 2; press seams toward A squares. Repeat to make four X rows.

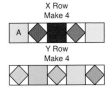

Figure 2

2. Join two A squares with three Square-in-a-Square blocks to make a Y row again referring to Figure 2; press seams toward A squares. Repeat to make four Y rows.

3. Arrange and join the X and Y rows referring to the Placement Diagram to complete the pieced center; press seams in one direction.

4. Sew a C strip to opposite long sides and D strips to the top and bottom of the pieced center; press seams toward C and D strips.

5. Join five each A and B squares to make a side row; press seams toward A squares. Repeat to make two side rows.

6. Sew the side rows to opposite sides of the pieced center; press seams toward C strips.

7. Join three B squares and four A squares to make the top row; press seams toward A squares.

8. Sew a Square-in-a-Square block to each end of the top row to complete the strip; press seams toward the blocks.

9. Repeat steps 7 and 8 with three A squares and four B squares to make the bottom row.

10. Sew the top and bottom rows to the pieced center to complete the pieced top; press seams toward D strips.

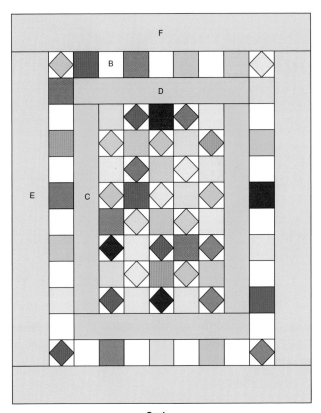

Spring
Placement Diagram 53½" x 67"

11. Join the E/F strips on short ends to make one long strip; press seams open. Subcut strip into two 54½" E strips and two 54" F strips. ***Note:*** *Mark strips with size since there is just a ½" difference. It would be easy to mix up the strips.*

12. Sew an E strip to opposite long sides and F strips to the top and bottom of the pieced center to complete the pieced top; press seams toward E and F strips.

13. Layer, quilt and bind referring to Finishing Your Quilt on page 173. ✤

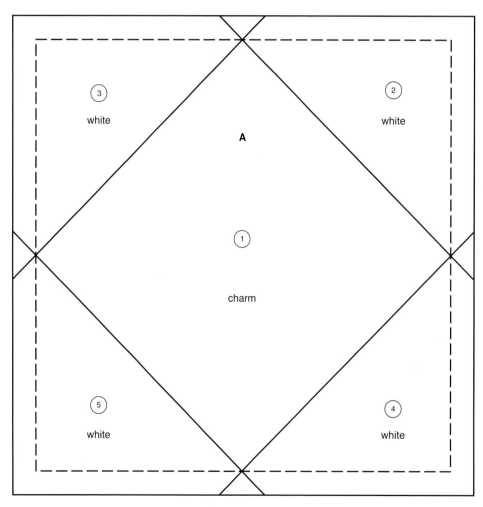

Paper-Piecing Pattern
Make 24 copies

Color Splash

Bright primary colors create a real splash in this flashy quilt.

Design by **JULIE WEAVER**

PROJECT SPECIFICATIONS

Skill Level: Beginner
Quilt Size: 52" x 64"
Block Size: 12" x 12"
Number of Blocks: 12

MATERIALS

- ¼ yard blue tonal
- ¼ yard orange stripe
- ¼ yard orange print
- ¼ yard light green tonal
- ¼ yard blue dot
- ⅓ yard blue print
- ⅓ yard red print
- ⅓ yard medium green tonal
- ⅜ yard red dot
- ⅜ yard yellow print
- ½ yard aqua dot
- 1⅔ yards bright blue print
- Batting 58" x 70"
- Backing 58" x 70"
- All-purpose thread to match fabrics
- Quilting thread
- Basic sewing tools and supplies

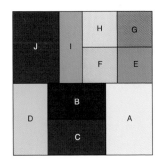

Splash
12" x 12" Block
Make 12

Cutting

1. Cut two 4½" by fabric width strips yellow print; subcut strips into (12) 6½" A pieces.

2. Cut two 3½" by fabric width B strips blue print.

3. Cut two 3½" by fabric width C strips red print.

4. Cut two 3½" by fabric width strips medium green tonal; subcut strips into (12) 6½" D rectangles.

5. Cut one 3½" by fabric width E strip blue tonal.

6. Cut one 3½" by fabric width F strip orange stripe.

7. Cut one 3½" by fabric width G strip orange print.

8. Cut one 3½" by fabric width H strip light green tonal.

9. Cut two 2½" by fabric width I strips blue dot.

10. Cut two 4½" by fabric width J strips red dot.

11. Cut three 2½" by fabric width K strips bright blue print.

12. Cut two 2½" x 40½" L strips bright blue print.

13. Cut six 4½" by fabric width O/P strips bright blue print.

14. Cut six 2¼" by fabric width strips bright blue print for binding.

15. Cut five 2½" by fabric width M/N strips aqua dot.

Completing the Blocks

1. Sew a B strip to a C strip along length to make a B-C strip set; press seam toward B. Repeat to make two strip sets.

2. Subcut the B-C strip sets into (12) 5½" B-C units as shown in Figure 1.

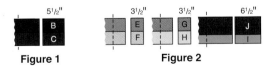

Figure 1   **Figure 2**

3. Sew an E strip to an F strip along length to make an E-F strip set; press seam toward E.

4. Subcut the E-F strip set into (12) 3½" E-F units as shown in Figure 2.

5. Repeat steps 3 and 4 with the G and H strips to make (12) 3½" G-H units pressing seam toward H, again referring to Figure 2.

6. Sew an I strip to a J strip along length to make an I-J strip set; press seam toward J. Repeat to make two I-J strip sets.

7. Subcut I-J strip sets into (12) 6½" I-J units, again referring to Figure 2.

8. To complete one Splash block, sew an E-F unit to a G-H unit to make a Four-Patch unit as shown in Figure 3; press seam in one direction.

Figure 3   Figure 4

9. Sew the Four-Patch unit to an I-J unit as shown in Figure 4; press seam toward I.

10. Sew a B-C unit between D and A as shown in Figure 5; press seams toward A and D.

Figure 5   Figure 6

11. Join the two pieced units to complete one Splash block referring to Figure 6; press seam in one direction.

12. Repeat steps 8–11 to complete 12 Splash block.

Completing the Top

1. Join three Splash blocks to make a row as shown in Figure 7; press seams in one direction. Repeat to make four rows.

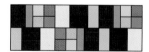

Figure 7

2. Join the rows referring to the Placement Diagram for positioning of rows to complete the pieced center; press seams in one direction.

3. Join the K strips on the short ends to make one long strip; press seams open. Subcut strip into two 48½" K strips.

4. Sew a K strip to opposite long sides and L strips to the top and bottom of the pieced center; press seams toward K and L strips.

5. Join the M/N strips on short ends to make one long strip; press seams open. Subcut strip into two 52½" M strips and two 44½" N strips.

6. Sew M strips to opposite long sides and N strips to the top and bottom of the pieced center; press seams toward M and N strips.

7. Join the O/P strips on short ends to make one long strip; press seams open. Subcut strip into two 56½" O strips and two 52½" P strips.

8. Sew the O strips to opposite long sides and P strips to the top and bottom of the pieced center; press seams toward O and P strips.

9. Layer, quilt and bind referring to Finishing Your Quilt on page 173. ❖

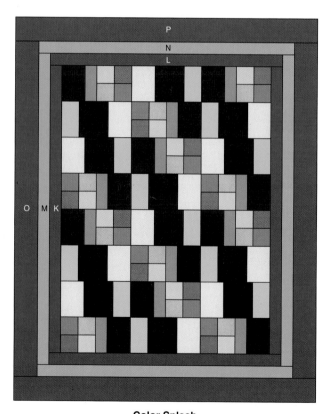

Color Splash
Placement Diagram 52" x 64"

Woodland Acres

Combine precut fabrics in the colors of the forest to make this masculine-looking quilt.

Design by **JULIA DUNN**

PROJECT SPECIFICATIONS

Skill Level: Beginner
Quilt Size: 73" x 73"
Block Size: 6" x 6"
Number of Blocks: 81

MATERIALS

- 1 charm pack or (40) 4½" x 4½" A squares
- 1 Jelly Roll™ or (40) 2½" x 42" strips in predominantly beige/black/brown tones
- ⅝ yard tan leaf print
- ⅞ yard tan animal print
- 1⅞ yards brown mottled
- Batting 79" x 79"
- Backing 79" x 79"
- Neutral-color all-purpose thread
- Quilting thread
- Basic sewing tools and supplies

Cutting

1. Trim each charm square to a 4½" x 4½" A square.

2. Cut seven 1½" by fabric width G/H strips tan animal print.

3. Cut two 6½" by fabric width strips tan animal print; subcut strips into (11) 6½" F1 squares.

4. Cut one 2½" by fabric width strip tan animal print; subcut strip into one 4½" B, one 6½" C and two 6½" D strips.

5. Cut two 6½" by fabric width strips tan leaf print; subcut strips into (11) 6½" F2 squares.

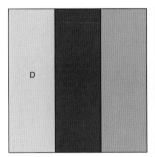

Strip
6" x 6" Block
Make 41

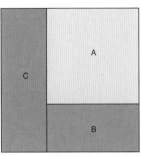

Frame
6" x 6" Block
Make 40

6. Cut one 2½" by fabric width strip tan leaf print; subcut strip into one each 4½" B, 6½" C and 6½" D strips.

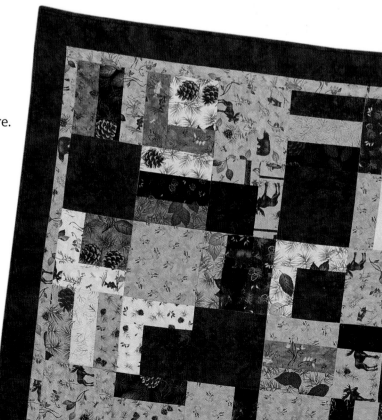

7. Cut 120 total 6½" D pieces from the (40) 2½" x 42" strips.

8. Subcut the remainder of the 2½" x 42" strips into 38 sets total of matching 4½" B and 6½" C pieces.

9. Cut three 6½" by fabric width strips brown mottled; subcut strips into (18) 6½" E squares.

10. Cut seven 3" by fabric width I/J strips brown mottled.

11. Cut eight 2¼" by fabric width strips brown mottled for binding.

Completing the Strip Blocks

1. Select three different D strips.

2. Join the strips along length; press seams in one direction to complete one Strip block.

3. Repeat steps 1 and 2 to complete 41 Strip blocks.

Completing the Frame Blocks

1. Select matching B and C pieces and one A square.

2. Sew B to A as shown in Figure 1; press seam toward B.

Figure 1

3. Add C to the left side of the A-B unit referring to Figure 1; press seam toward C to complete one Frame block.

4. Repeat steps 1–3 to complete 40 Frame blocks.

Completing the Top

1. Referring to Figure 2, select and join blocks with E and F squares to complete rows; press seams in adjacent rows in opposite directions.

2. Join the rows as arranged, again referring to Figure 2; press seams in one direction.

3. Join the G/H strips on short ends to make one long strip; press seams open. Subcut strip into two 66½" G strips and two 68½" H strips.

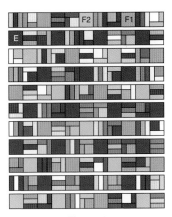

Figure 2

4. Sew G strips to opposite sides and H strips to the top and bottom of the pieced center; press seams toward G and H strips.

5. Join the I/J strips on short ends to make one long strip; press seams open. Subcut strip into two 68½" I strips and two 73½" J strips.

6. Sew I strips to opposite sides and J strips to the top and bottom of the pieced center; press seams toward I and J strips to complete the pieced top.

7. Layer, quilt and bind referring to Finishing Your Quilt on page 173. ❖

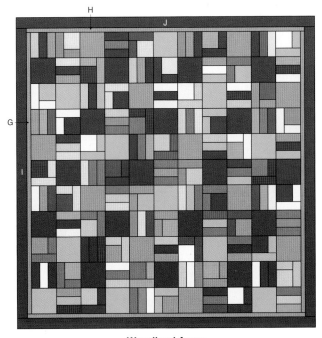

Woodland Acres
Placement Diagram 73" x 73"

Long Logs

Elongated Log Cabin blocks create an easy-to-stitch quilt.

Design by **CONNIE EWBANK**

PROJECT SPECIFICATIONS

Skill Level: Beginner
Quilt Size: 46" x 56"
Block Size: 10" x 10"
Number of Blocks: 20

MATERIALS

- ⅛ yard medium/dark green (B)
- ¼ yard dark green (D)
- ¼ yard medium rose (F)
- ⅓ yard light gold (GL)
- ⅓ yard medium gold (GM)
- ⅓ yard light rose (H)
- ½ yard medium teal/blue (A)
- ½ yard medium/light teal (C)
- ⅝ yard medium/light green (E)
- ⅝ yard burgundy (I)
- ⅝ yard dark green tonal
- ⅝ yard medium green floral (J/K)
- Batting 52" x 62"
- Backing 52" x 62"
- Neutral-color all-purpose thread
- Quilting thread
- Basic sewing tools and supplies

Cutting

1. Cut seven 1½" by fabric width strips medium teal/blue; subcut strips into (40) 6½" A strips.

2. Cut two 1½" by fabric width strips medium/dark green; subcut strips into (40) 1½" B squares.

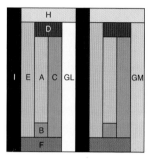

Elongated Log Cabin
10" x 10" Block
Make 20

3. Cut eight 1½" by fabric width strips medium/light teal; subcut strips into (40) 7½" C strips.

4. Cut three 1½" by fabric width strips dark green; subcut strips into (40) 2½" D pieces.

5. Cut (10) 1½" by fabric width strips medium/light green; subcut strips into (40) 8½" E strips.

6. Cut four 1½" by fabric width strips medium rose; subcut strips into (40) 3½" F pieces.

7. Cut five 1½" by fabric width strips light gold; subcut strips into (20) 9½" GL strips.

8. Cut five 1½" by fabric width strips medium gold; subcut strips into (20) 9½" GM strips.

9. Cut five 1½" by fabric width strips light rose; subcut strips into (40) 4½" H pieces.

10. Cut (10) 1½" by fabric width strips burgundy; subcut strips into (40) 10½" I strips.

11. Cut five 3½" by fabric width J/K strips medium green floral.

12. Cut six 2¼" by fabric width strips dark green tonal for binding.

Completing the Blocks

Note: Press seams away from the center strip after the addition of each new piece. Use a ¼" seam allowance throughout.

1. To complete one Elongated Log Cabin block, sew B to one end of A and add C to complete an A-B-C unit as shown in Figure 1; press.

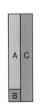

Figure 1

Figure 2

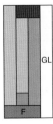

Figure 3

2. Add D to the top and E to the left side of the A-B-C unit as shown in Figure 2; press.

3. Add F to the bottom and GL to the right side as shown in Figure 3; press.

4. Add H to the top and I to the left side to complete half of the block as shown in Figure 4; press.

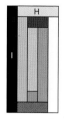
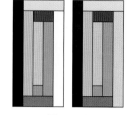

Figure 4   Figure 5

5. Repeat steps 1–4 using GM instead of GL to complete the second half of the block.

6. Join the two block halves as shown in Figure 5 to complete one Elongated Log Cabin block; press.

7. Repeat steps 1–6 to complete 20 Elongated Log Cabin blocks.

Completing the Top

1. Join four Elongated Log Cabin blocks to make an X row as shown in Figure 6; press seams in one direction. Repeat to make three X rows.

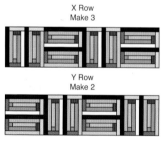

X Row
Make 3

Y Row
Make 2

Figure 6

2. Join four Elongated Log Cabin blocks to make a Y row, again referring to Figure 6; press seams in the opposite direction from the X row. Repeat to make two Y rows.

3. Join the X and Y rows referring to the Placement Diagram for positioning of rows; press seams in one direction.

4. Join the J/K strips with right sides together on short ends to make one long strip; press seams

open. Subcut strip into two 50½" J strips and two 46½" K strips.

5. Sew J strips to opposite long sides and K strips to the top and bottom of the pieced center; press seams toward J and K strips to complete the pieced top.

6. Layer, quilt and bind referring to Finishing Your Quilt on page 173. ❖

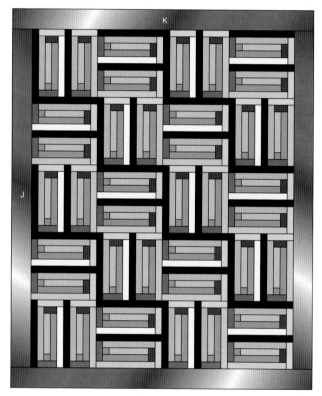

Long Logs
Placement Diagram 46" x 56"

Tip **If you always stitch with the pieced unit on top,** you will be less likely to flip a seam in the wrong direction. Always press between each addition of a strip to the unit, press seams away from the center strip.

Uncommon Quilts

Traditional quilts are made of blocks, but that isn't true of many quilts you see today. In fact, in some quilt designs it is difficult to tell where one block stops and the next one starts. Other quilts have an off-center design or a secondary design that you can only find with a close second look.

Cabin in the Orchard

An apple print is the focal fabric in this off-center
Log Cabin–design quilt.

Design by **BRENDA CONNELLY & BARB MILLER FOR BRENDABARB DESIGNS**

PROJECT SPECIFICATIONS

Skill Level: Beginner
Quilt Size: 56" x 71"
Block Size: 15" x 15"
Number of Blocks: 12

MATERIALS

- ¼ yard each 6 different white/cream
  (L-light) fabrics
- ¼ yard each 6 different red/burgundy
  (D-dark) fabrics
- ¼ yard green mottled
- ⅜ yard black solid
- 2 yards apple print (A) (2⅜ yards if directional)
- Batting 62" x 77"
- Backing 62" x 77"
- All-purpose thread to match fabrics
- Quilting thread
- Basic sewing tools and supplies

Cutting

1. Cut two pieces in each of the following sizes
from each of the six L fabrics: 3" x 3½" L1, 3" x 6" L2,
2½" x 8½" L3, 2½" x 10½" L4, 2" x 12½" L5 and
2" x 14" L6.

2. Cut two pieces in each of the following sizes
from each of the six D fabrics: 3" x 3½" D1 pieces,
3" x 6" D2, 2½" x 8½" D3, 2½" x 10½" D4, 2" x 12½"
D5 and 2" x 14" D6.

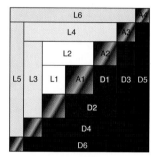

Apple Log
15" x 15" Block
Make 12

3. Cut one 3½" by fabric width strip apple print;
subcut strip into (12) 3½" A1 squares.

4. Cut two 3" by fabric width strips apple print;
subcut strips into (24) 3" A2 squares.

5. Cut two 2½" by fabric width strips apple print;
subcut strips into (24) 2½" A3 squares.

6. Cut two 2" by fabric width strips apple print;
subcut strips into (24) 2" A4 squares.

7. Cut six 4½" by fabric width E/F strips apple print.
Note: *If using a directional print, cut two 4½" x63½" E
strips along the length of the fabric, and then cut four
4½" x 33" F strips across the remaining width.*

8. Cut seven 2¼" by fabric width strips apple
print for binding.

9. Cut six 1" by fabric width A/B strips
green mottled.

10. Cut six 1½" by fabric width C/D strips black solid.

Completing the Apple Log Blocks

1. To complete one Apple Log block, select one matching set each L1/L2, L3/L4, L5/L6, D1/D2, D3/D4 and D5/D6 pieces.

2. Sew an L1 and D1 piece to opposite sides of A1 to make the center row; press seams away from L1.

3. Sew an A2 square to one end of one each L2 and D2 piece as shown in Figure 1; press seams toward A2.

Figure 1

4. Sew the L2-A2 strip to the top and the A2-D2 strip to the bottom of the center row as shown in Figure 2; press seams away from the center row.

Figure 2

5. Sew L3 to the L1 side and D3 to the D1 side of the pieced unit as shown in Figure 3; press seams toward L3 and D3.

Figure 3

6. Sew an A3 square to one end of one each L4 and D4 pieces; press seams toward A3.

7. Sew the L4-A3 strip to the L2 side and the D4-A3 strip to the D2 side of the pieced unit as shown in Figure 4; press seams away from the pieced unit.

Figure 4

8. Sew L5 to the L3 side and D5 to the D3 side of the pieced unit referring to the block drawing; press seams toward L5 and D5 strips.

9. Sew an A4 square to one end of one each L6 and D6 pieces; press seams toward A4.

10. Sew an L6-A4 strip to the L4 side and a D6-A4 strip to the D4 side of the pieced unit to complete one Apple Log block referring to the block drawing; press seams toward the L6-A4 and D6-A4 strips.

11. Repeat steps 1–10 to complete 12 Apple Log blocks.

Completing the Top

1. Arrange and join three blocks to make a row as shown in Figure 5; press seams in one direction.

Figure 5

2. Repeat step 1 with three blocks to make three different rows referring to Figure 6; press seams in adjacent rows in opposite directions.

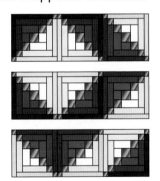

Figure 6

3. Join the rows as arranged and referring to the Placement Diagram; press seams in one direction.

4. Join the A/B strips on short ends to make one long strip; press seams open. Subcut strip into two 60½" A strips and two 46½" B strips.

5. Sew an A strip to opposite long sides and B strips to the top and bottom of the pieced center; press seams toward A and B strips.

6. Repeat step 4 with C/D strips; subcut strip into two 61½" C strips and two 48½" D strips.

7. Sew a C strip to opposite long sides and D strips to the top and bottom of the pieced center; press seams toward C and D strips.

8. Repeat step 4 with E/F strips; subcut strip into two 63½" E strips and two 56½" F strips. ***Note:*** *If E/F fabric is directional, join the four previously cut F strips as in step 4 and cut to size for F.*

9. Sew an E strip to opposite long sides and F strips to the top and bottom of the pieced center; press seams toward E and F strips to complete the pieced top.

10. Layer, quilt and bind referring to Finishing Your Quilt on page 173. ❖

Cabin in the Orchard
Placement Diagram 56" x 71"

Luscious Jiffy Cake Quilt & Pillow Shams

Use luscious Layer Cakes™ and Jelly Rolls™ to make this beautiful, yet simple quilt set.

Designs by JULIE HIGGINS

PROJECT SPECIFICATIONS

Skill Level: Beginner
Quilt Size: 104" x 113"
Sham Size: 41" x 27½"

MATERIALS

- 28 (10" x 10") Layer Cake squares for A (or cut your own)
- 2 Jelly Rolls or 80 (2½" x 42") fabric strips to coordinate with Layer Cakes
- 7⅝ yards black solid
- Batting 110" x 119" for quilt
- 2 batting pieces 47" x 34" for shams
- Backing 110" x 119" for quilt
- 4 backing pieces 30" x 28" for shams
- 2 (47" x 34") pieces muslin for sham linings
- All-purpose thread to match fabrics
- Quilting thread
- Basic sewing tools and supplies

Quilt

Cutting

1. Cut the 2½" x 42" Jelly Roll strips into random lengths.

2. Cut six 14¾" by fabric width strips black solid; subcut strips into (11) 14¾" B squares and six 7⅝" C squares. Cut each B square on both diagonals to make 44 B triangles. Cut each C square in half on one diagonal to make 12 C triangles.

3. Cut two 7⅝" by fabric width strips black solid; subcut strips into six 7⅝" squares. Cut each square in half on one diagonal to make 12 C triangles (to total 24 with those cut in step 2).

4. Cut (11) 2¼" by fabric width strips black solid for binding.

5. Cut four 3½" x 35½" J strips and four 3½" x 28" K strips black solid.

6. Cut two 10½" x 93½" F strips and two 10½" x 104½" G strips along the remaining length of black solid.

Completing the Quilt Top

1. Sew a B triangle to opposite sides of 16 A squares as shown in Figure 1; press seams toward B.

Figure 1

2. Sew a C triangle to two adjacent sides of an A square and add a B triangle to one of the remaining sides to make A-B-C end units as shown in Figure 2. Repeat to make eight end units for quilt and four for shams.

Figure 2

3. Join four A-B units with two end units to complete an A row as shown in Figure 3; press seams in one direction. Repeat to make four A rows.

Figure 3

4. Join randomly selected cut Jelly Roll lengths on the short ends to make (15) 84" D strips.

5. Join three D strips along length to make a strip row; press seams in one direction. Trim strip to 81½"; repeat to make five D rows.

6. Join the A rows with the D rows referring to the Placement Diagram; press seams toward D rows.

7. Repeat steps 4 and 5 to make six 86" E strips; join three strips, press and trim to 84½" to make two E rows.

8. Sew an E row to the top and bottom of the pieced center; press seams toward E rows.

9. Sew an F strip to opposite long sides and G strips to the top and bottom of the pieced center; press seams toward F and G strips to complete the pieced top.

10. Layer, quilt and bind referring to Finishing Your Quilt on page 173.

Pillow Shams

Completing the Sham Tops

1. To complete the pillow sham tops, join two end units (made with the quilt end units) to

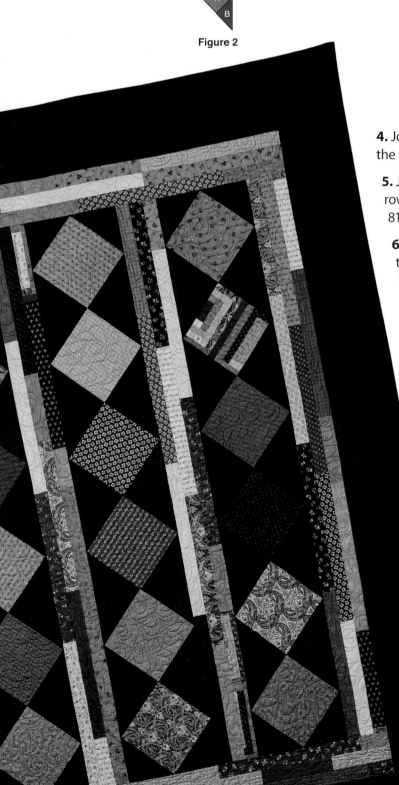

complete one sham center; press seam in one direction. Repeat to make two sham centers.

2. Join randomly selected cut Jelly Roll lengths on short ends to make three 160"-long strips; press seams in one direction.

3. Subcut the stitched strips into eight 14" H strips and eight 35½" I strips.

4. Join two H strips along length to make an H end strip; press. Repeat to make four H end strips. Press seams in one direction.

5. Repeat step 4 with I strips to make four I side strips.

6. Sew an H end strip to opposite short ends and I side strips to opposite long sides of each sham center; press seams toward H and I strips.

7. Sew J strips to opposite long sides and K strips to the short ends of each sham center to complete two sham tops; press seams toward J and K strips.

Completing the Shams

1. Sandwich a 47" x 34" piece of batting between a completed sham top and a 47" x 34" piece of muslin; pin or baste layers together to hold.

2. Quilt as desired by hand or machine; remove pins or basting. Trim excess lining and batting even with quilt top.

3. Turn under one 28" edge on each of two sham backing pieces ¼"; press. Turn under again, press and stitch to hem.

4. Place the two backing pieces right sides together with a sham top, overlapping hemmed edges as shown in Figure 4; stitch all around.

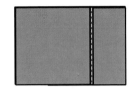

Figure 4

5. Clip corners; turn right side out through opening. Press edges flat.

6. Stitch in the ditch between the H and K strips, and the I and J strips to make a flange on the edges.

7. Repeat steps 1–6 to complete two pillow shams. ✤

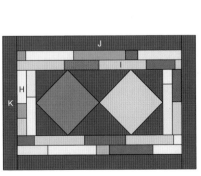

Luscious Jiffy Cake Pillow Sham
Placement Diagram 41" x 27½"

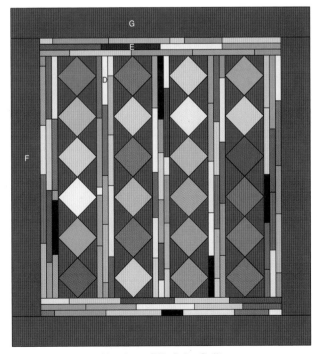

Luscious Jiffy Cake Quilt
Placement Diagram 104" x 113"

Interlocking Blocks

The strips and squares of this quilt are a puzzle in the making.

Design by **ANN ANDERSON**

PROJECT SPECIFICATIONS

Skill Level: Intermediate
Quilt Size: 53" x 53"
Block Sizes: 14½" x 14½", 13" x 14½" and 13" x 13"
Number of Blocks: 4, 1 and 4

MATERIALS

- ¼ yard purple print
- ⅓ yard rust tonal
- ½ yard yellow tonal
- ½ yard purple tonal
- 1¼ yards lengthwise coordinating stripe
- 1½ yards blue tonal
- Batting 59" x 59"
- Backing 59" x 59"
- All-purpose thread to match fabrics
- Quilting thread
- Basic sewing tools and supplies

Cutting

1. Cut one 3½" by fabric width strip purple print; subcut strip into nine 3½" A squares. ***Note:*** *If the fabric has special motifs, you may fussy-cut these squares from the fabric.*

2. Cut one 4" by fabric width strip coordinating stripe; subcut strips into (12) 3½" B pieces. ***Note:*** *See the Alternate Cutting sidebar on page 75 for cutting stripe printed across the width.*

3. Cut two 5½" by fabric width strip coordinating stripe; subcut strip into (20) 3½" C pieces.

4. Cut one 7" by fabric width strips coordinating stripe; subcut strip into four 3½" D pieces.

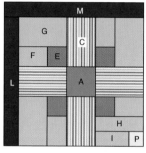

Purple Interlocking
14½" x 14½" Block
Make 4

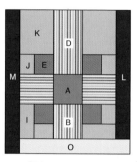

Side Interlocking
13" x 14½" Block
Make 4

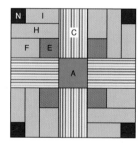

Center Interlocking
13" x 13" Block
Make 1

5. Cut six 2¼" by fabric width strips coordinating stripe for binding.

6. Cut three 2½" by fabric width strips rust tonal; subcut strip into (36) 2½" E squares.

7. Cut three 3½" by fabric width strips blue tonal; subcut strip into (20) 2½" F pieces and (12) 5½" G pieces.

8. Cut four 2" by fabric width strips blue tonal; subcut strips into eight 5½" H pieces, (16) 4" I pieces and (16) 2½" J pieces.

9. Cut one 4" by fabric width strip blue tonal; subcut strip into eight 5" K pieces.

10. Cut five 5" by fabric width S/T strips blue tonal.

11. Cut six 2" by fabric width strips purple tonal; subcut strips into eight 13½" L strips, eight 15" M strips and four 2" N squares.

12. Cut two 2" by fabric width strips yellow tonal; subcut strips into four 12" O pieces and four 2" P squares.

13. Cut five 1½" by fabric width Q/R strips yellow tonal.

Completing the Center Interlocking Block

1. Sew E to F and N to I; press seams toward E and N.

2. Sew H between the E-F and I-N units to complete a corner unit as shown in Figure 1; repeat to make four corner units.

 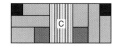

Figure 1   **Figure 2**

3. Join two corner units with C to make a C unit as shown in Figure 2; press seams toward C. Repeat to make two C units.

4. Sew A between two C pieces to complete an A unit; press seams toward C.

5. Sew a C unit to opposite sides of an A unit to complete the Center Interlocking block referring to the block drawing; press seams toward the A unit.

Completing the Purple Interlocking Blocks

1. Sew E to F and I to P; press seams toward E and P.

2. Sew H between the E-F and I-P units to complete a P corner unit as shown in Figure 3; press seams toward H.

Figure 3   **Figure 4**

3. Sew E to F and add G to make a G corner unit as shown in Figure 4; press seam toward G. Repeat to make three G corner units.

4. Join two G corner units with C to make a G row as shown in Figure 5; press seams toward C.

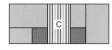

Figure 5

5. Join one G corner unit with the P corner unit and C to complete a P row as shown in Figure 6; press seam toward C.

Figure 6

6. Sew A between two C pieces to make an A row; press seams toward C.

7. Sew the A row between the G and P rows; press seams toward the A row.

8. Sew an L strip to the left side and the M strip to the top of the pieced unit to complete one Purple Interlocking block referring to the block drawing; press seams toward L and M strips.

9. Repeat steps 1–8 to complete four Purple Interlocking blocks.

Completing the Side Interlocking Blocks

1. Sew J to E and add K to make a K corner unit as shown in Figure 7; press seam toward K. Repeat to make two K corner units.

Figure 7

2. Sew J to E and add I to complete an I corner unit referring to Figure 8; press seam toward I. Repeat to make two I corner units.

Figure 8

3. Join the two K corner units with D to complete a D row as shown in Figure 9; press seams toward D.

Figure 9

4. Sew A between two B pieces to make an A row; press seams toward B.

5. Join the two I corner units with B to complete an E row as shown in Figure 10; press seams toward B.

Figure 10

6. Sew the A row between the D row and the E row referring to the block drawing; press seams toward the A row.

7. Sew an L strip to the right side of the pieced unit and O to the bottom referring to the block drawing; add M to the left side to complete one Side Interlocking block; press seams toward L, O and M.

8. Repeat steps 1–7 to complete four Side Interlocking blocks.

Completing the Top

1. Join two Purple Interlocking blocks with one Side Interlocking block to make a purple row as shown in Figure 11; press seams toward side blocks. Repeat to make two purple rows.

2. Join two Side Interlocking blocks with the Center Interlocking block to make the yellow row, again referring to Figure 11; press seams toward the Side Interlocking blocks.

Make 2

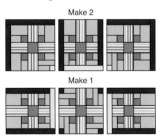

Make 1

Figure 11

3. Sew the yellow row between the two purple rows to complete the pieced center; press seams toward purple rows.

4. Join the Q/R strips on short ends to make one long strip; press seams open. Subcut strip into two 42½" Q strips and two 44½" R strips.

5. Sew a Q strip to opposite sides and R strips to the top and bottom of the pieced center; press seams toward Q and R strips.

6. Join the S/T strips on short ends to make one long strip; press seams open. Subcut strip into two 44½" S strips and two 53½" T strips.

7. Sew S strips to opposite sides and T strips to the top and bottom of the pieced center; press seams toward S and T strips to complete the pieced top.

8. Layer, quilt and bind referring to Finishing Your Quilt on page 173. ✤

Alternate Cutting

If your stripe is printed across the width of the fabric, cut six 3½" strips along the length of the fabric; subcut strips into (12) 4" B, (20) 5½" C and four 7" D pieces.

Cut six 2¼" binding strips along the length of the fabric.

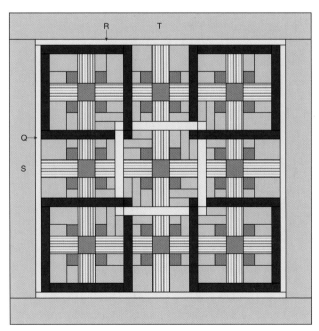

Interlocking Baby Quilt
Placement Diagram 53" x 53"

Gypsy Wind

Add pieced borders to two sides only to create a unique quilt.

Design by PHYLLIS DOBBS

PROJECT SPECIFICATIONS

Skill Level: Beginner
Quilt Size: 45" x 53"

MATERIALS

- ¼ yard light turquoise tonal
- ¼ yard medium green tonal
- ⅓ yard small turquoise print
- ⅜ yard multicolored medallion stripe
- ½ yard medium turquoise tonal
- ⅝ yard small turquoise medallion print
- ¾ yard purple print
- ¾ yard large multicolored print
- 1¼ yards light green tonal
- Batting 51" x 59"
- Backing 51" x 59"
- All-purpose thread to match fabrics
- Quilting thread
- Basic sewing tools and supplies

Cutting

1. Cut one 5½" by fabric width strip light turquoise tonal; subcut strip into two 5½" A squares.

2. Cut one 5½" by fabric width strip medium turquoise tonal; subcut strip into two 5½" B squares.

3. Cut two 1½" x 38½" M strips and two 1½" x 32½" N strips medium turquoise tonal.

4. Cut one 5⅞" by fabric width strip light green tonal; subcut strip into four 5⅞" squares. Cut each square in half on one diagonal to make eight C triangles.

5. Cut two 2" x 30½" G strips light green tonal.

6. Cut two 4⅞" by fabric width strips light green tonal; subcut strips into (10) 4⅞" squares. Cut each square in half on one diagonal to make 20 P triangles.

7. Cut one 4½" by fabric width strip light green tonal; subcut strip into four 4½" R squares.

8. Cut five 2¼" by fabric width strips light green tonal for binding.

9. Cut one 5⅞" by fabric width strip purple print; subcut strip into six 5⅞" squares. Cut each square in half on one diagonal to make 12 D triangles.

10. Cut two 4⅞" by fabric width strips purple print; subcut strips into (10) 4⅞" squares. Cut each square in half on one diagonal to make 20 Q triangles.

11. Cut one 6¼" by fabric width strip purple print; subcut strip into three 6¼" squares. Cut each square on both diagonals to make 12 J triangles.

12. Cut one 5½" by fabric width strip large multicolored print; subcut strip into seven 5½" E squares.

13. Cut one 5⅞" by fabric width strip large multicolored print; subcut strip into two 5⅞" squares and one 5½" x 5½" E square (to total eight). Cut the two 5⅞" x 5⅞" squares in half on one diagonal to make four F triangles.

14. Cut two 4½" x 30½" L strips large multicolored print.

15. Cut two 1½" x 30½" H strips medium green tonal.

16. Cut one 3" by fabric width strip medium green tonal; subcut strip into four 3" U squares.

17. Cut one 6¼" by fabric width strip small turquoise print; subcut strip into three 6¼" squares and two 3⅜" x 3⅜" squares. Cut the larger squares on both diagonals to make 12 I triangles (discard two) and the smaller squares in half on one diagonal to make four K triangles.

18. Cut two 3" x 40½" S strips small turquoise medallion print.

19. Cut three 3" by fabric width T strips small turquoise medallion print.

20. Cut two 4½" x 32½" O strips multicolored medallion stripe with large medallions centered.

Completing the Top

1. Sew an A square to a B square; repeat. Press seams toward B.

2. Join the A-B units to complete the center unit; press seam in one direction.

3. Sew C to D along the diagonal to make a C-D unit; press seam toward D. Repeat to make eight C-D units.

4. Join two C-D units as shown in Figure 1; press seam in one direction. Repeat to make four joined units.

Figure 1

5. Sew a joined unit to opposite sides of the center unit as shown in Figure 2; press seams toward the center unit.

Figure 2

6. Sew E to each end of the two remaining joined units as shown in Figure 3; press seams toward E. Sew these units to the top and bottom of the center unit as shown in Figure 4; press seams away from the center unit.

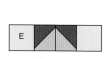

Figure 3   **Figure 4**

7. Sew D to F along the diagonal to make a D-F unit; press seam toward D. Repeat to make four D-F units.

8. Join two E squares with two D-F units to complete a D-F-E strip as shown in Figure 5; press seams toward E squares. Repeat to make two D-F-E strips.

Figure 5

9. Sew a D-F-E strip to opposite sides of the pieced center unit as shown in Figure 6 to complete the pieced center; press seams toward the D-F-E strips.

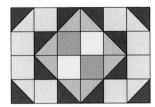

Figure 6

10. Sew a G strip and then an H strip to the top and bottom of the pieced center; press seams toward G and then H.

11. Sew I to J as shown in Figure 7; press seam toward J. Repeat to make 10 I-J units.

Figure 7   **Figure 8**

12. Join five I-J units, one J triangle and two K triangles as shown in Figure 8 to make an I-J-K strip; press seams in one direction. Repeat to make two I-J-K strips.

13. Sew an I-J-K strip to the top and bottom of the pieced center referring to the Placement Diagram for positioning; press seams toward H strips.

14. Sew an L strip to the top and bottom of the pieced center; press seams toward L strips.

15. Sew an M strip to opposite long sides and N strips to the top and bottom of the pieced center; press seams toward M and N strips.

16. Sew an O strip to the top and bottom of the pieced center; press seams toward N strips.

17. Sew P to Q along the diagonal to make a P-Q unit; press seam toward Q. Repeat to make 20 P-Q units.

18. Join two P-Q units as shown in Figure 9 to make a side unit; press seam in one direction. Repeat to make 10 side units.

Figure 9

19. Join five side units with two R squares to make a side strip referring to the Placement Diagram for positioning; press seams toward R and then in one direction. Repeat to make two side strips.

20. Sew a side strip to opposite sides of the pieced center referring to the Placement Diagram for positioning; press seams toward M strips.

21. Sew an S strip to the top and bottom of the pieced center; press seams toward S strips.

22. Join the T strips on short ends to make one long strip; press seams open. Subcut strip into two 48½" T strips.

23. Sew a U square to each end of each T strip; press seams toward T strips.

24. Sew a T-U strip to opposite long sides of the pieced center; press seams toward the T-U strip to complete the pieced top.

25. Layer, quilt and bind referring to Finishing Your Quilt on page 173. ❖

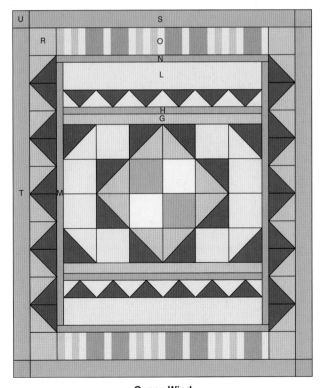

Gypsy Wind
Placement Diagram 45" x 53"

Salad

Four large blocks make up the center of this bright throw.

Design by **CHRISTINE SCHULTZ**

PROJECT SPECIFICATIONS

Skill Level: Beginner
Quilt Size: 65" x 65"
Block Size: 26" x 26"
Number of Blocks: 4

MATERIALS

- 16 fat quarters assorted prints
- 1⅛ yards green print
- Batting 71" x 71"
- Backing 71" x 71"
- Neutral-color all-purpose thread
- Quilting thread
- Basic sewing tools and supplies

Cutting

1. Refer to Figure 1 for cutting to make best use of fabrics. You will need (32) 4½" x 4½" A squares, (40) 4½" x 6½" B pieces, (16) 6½" x 8½" C pieces, (20) 6½"

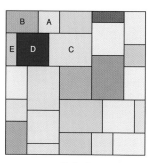

Salad
26" x 26" Block
Make 4

x 6½" D pieces, (40) 2½" x 6½" E pieces, four 4½" x 8½" H pieces and four 4½" x 7½" I pieces.

2. Cut six 3" by fabric width F/G strips green print.

3. Cut seven 2¼" by fabric width strips green print for binding.

Completing the Blocks

Note: *Use a ¼" seam allowance throughout.*

1. To complete one Salad block, sew A between two B rectangles as shown in Figure 2; press seams in one direction.

Figure 2

2. Sew C to D to E as shown in Figure 3; press seams toward E.

Figure 3

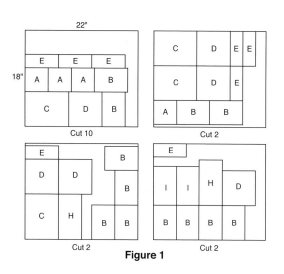

Figure 1

3. Join the A-B unit and the C-D-E unit with seams going in opposite directions to complete one block unit; press seam toward the C-D-E unit.

4. Repeat steps 1–3 to complete four block units.

5. Sew a D square to the C end of one block unit, stopping stitching 1½" from end as shown in Figure 4; press seam away from D.

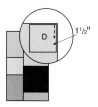

Figure 4

6. Sew a second pieced unit to an adjacent side of D as shown in Figure 5; press seam away from D.

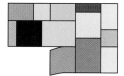

Figure 5

7. Add a third pieced unit as in step 6; press seam away from D.

8. Add the final pieced unit to the side of D with the partial seam; press seam away from D.

9. Complete the partial seam as shown in Figure 6 to complete one Salad block; press seam away from D and toward the first unit.

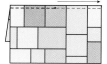

Figure 6

10. Repeat steps 1–9 to complete four blocks.

Completing the Top

1. Join the F/G strips on short ends to make one long strip; press seams open. Subcut strip into two 52½" F strips and two 57½" G strips.

2. Sew an F strip to opposite sides and G strips to the top and bottom of the pieced center; press seams toward F and G strips.

3. Join two E pieces on the long edges to make an E unit; press seam to one side. Repeat to make 12 E units.

4. Join three A, two B and one each H and I pieces with three E units to make a right-side strip as shown in Figure 7; press seams in one direction.

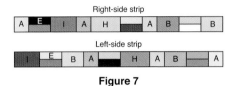

Right-side strip

Left-side strip

Figure 7

5. Repeat step 4 to make the left-side strip, again referring to Figure 7; press seams in one direction.

6. Sew the side strips to the appropriate sides of the pieced center referring to the Placement Diagram for positioning; press seams toward the F strips.

7. Join five A, two B, one each H and I pieces with three E units to make the top strip referring to Figure 8; press seams away from end A pieces and in one direction for remainder of strip. Sew the strip to the top of the pieced center; press seam toward G strip.

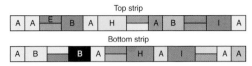

Top strip

Bottom strip

Figure 8

8. Repeat step 7 to make the bottom strip, again referring to Figure 8; press seams as in step 7. Sew the strip to the bottom of the pieced center; press seams toward G strip to complete the top.

9. Layer, quilt and bind referring to Finishing Your Quilt on page 173. ❖

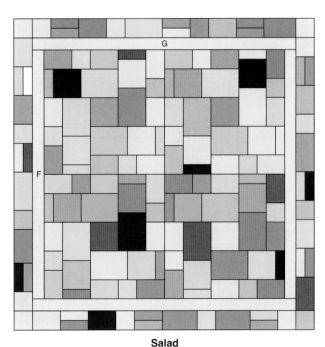

Salad
Placement Diagram 65" x 65"

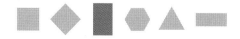

Well-Connected Stars

The stars in this quilt are interconnected by colors.

Design by JUDITH SANDSTROM

PROJECT SPECIFICATIONS

Skill Level: Advanced
Quilt Size: 66" x 84"
Block Size: 12" x 12"
Number of Blocks: 28

MATERIALS

- ¼ yard each 4 blue stripes
- ⅓ yard green tonal
- ⅓ yard purple tonal
- ⅓ yard each 4 blue prints
- ½ yard each 4 yellow prints
- ⅔ yard cream/multicolored stripe
- 1¼ yards blue tonal
- 1⅜ yards orange print
- 1½ yards yellow tonal
- Batting 72" x 90"
- Backing 72" x 90"
- Neutral-color all-purpose thread
- Quilting thread
- Basic sewing tools and supplies

Cutting

1. Cut three 4¾" by fabric width strips yellow tonal; subcut strips into (24) 4¾" A squares.

2. Cut five 3⅞" by fabric width strips yellow tonal; subcut strips into (42) 3⅞" squares. Cut each square in half on one diagonal to make 84 G triangles.

3. Cut four 3½" by fabric width strips yellow tonal; subcut strips into (48) 3½" H squares.

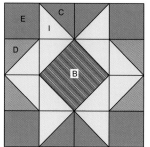

Blue/Yellow
12" x 12" Block
Make 8

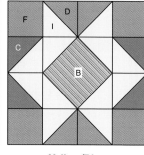

Yellow/Blue
12" x 12" Block
Make 8

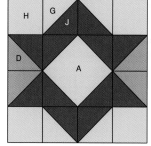

Yellow/Orange
12" x 12" Block
Make 4

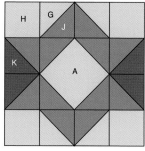

Yellow/Green
12" x 12" Block
Make 4

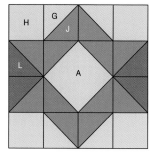

Yellow/Purple
12" x 12" Block
Make 4

4. Cut one 4¾" by fabric width strip each blue stripe; subcut strips into (25) 4¾" B squares total.

5. Cut seven 3⅞" by fabric width strips blue tonal; subcut strips into (68) 3⅞" squares. Cut each square in half on one diagonal to make 136 C triangles.

6. Cut three 3½" by fabric width strips blue tonal; subcut strips into (32) 3½" E squares.

7. Cut nine 3⅞" by fabric width strips orange print; subcut strips into (88) 3⅞" squares. Cut each square in half on one diagonal to make 176 D triangles.

8. Cut three 3½" by fabric width strips orange print; subcut strips into (32) 3½" F squares.

9. Cut three 3⅞" by fabric width strips each yellow print; subcut strips into (24) 3⅞" squares each fabric. Cut each square in half on one diagonal to make 48 I triangles each.

10. Cut two 3⅞" by fabric width strips each blue print; subcut strips into (18) 3⅞" squares each fabric. Cut each square in half on one diagonal to make 36 J triangles each.

11. Cut two 3⅞" by fabric width strips green tonal; subcut strips into (20) 3⅞" squares. Cut each square in half on one diagonal to make 40 K triangles.

12. Cut two 3⅞" by fabric width strips purple tonal; subcut strips into (20) 3⅞" squares. Cut each square in half on one diagonal to make 40 L triangles.

13. Cut eight 2¼" by fabric width strips cream/multicolored stripe for binding.

Completing the Blue/Yellow Blocks

Note: *Use a ¼" seam allowance throughout. Press all seams open unless otherwise directed.*

1. To make one Blue/Yellow block, select 12 matching I triangles and one B square.

2. Sew I to each side of B; press seams toward I.

3. Sew I to D along the diagonal to make a D-I unit as shown in Figure 1; press seam toward D. Repeat to make four D-I units. Repeat to make four C-I units, again referring to Figure 1.

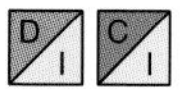

Figure 1 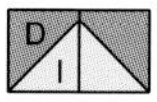   **Figure 2**

4. Join two D-I units to make a side unit as shown in Figure 2; press seam in one direction. Repeat to make two side units.

5. Sew a side unit to opposite sides of the B-I unit to complete the center row; press seams toward the B-I unit.

6. Join two C-I units and add E as shown in Figure 3 to make the top unit; press seams toward E. Repeat to make the bottom unit.

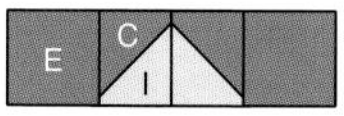

Figure 3

7. Sew the top and bottom units to the center row to complete one Blue/Yellow block as shown in Figure 4; press seams toward the center row.

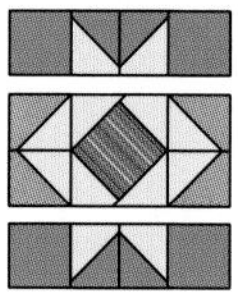

Figure 4

8. Repeat steps 1–7 to complete eight Blue/Yellow blocks.

Completing the Yellow/Blue Blocks

1. Using B, I, C, D and F pieces, complete eight Yellow/Blue blocks referring to Figure 5 and Completing the Blue/Yellow Blocks.

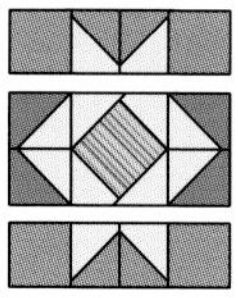

Figure 5

Completing the Yellow/Orange Blocks

1. Using A, D, H, G and J pieces, complete four Yellow/Orange blocks referring to Figure 6 and Completing the Blue/Yellow Blocks.

Figure 6

Completing the Yellow/Green Blocks

1. Using A, H, G, K and J pieces, complete four Yellow/Green blocks referring to Figure 7 and Completing the Blue/Yellow Blocks.

Figure 7

Completing the Yellow/Purple Blocks

1. Using A, H, G, J and L pieces, complete four Yellow/Purple blocks referring to Figure 8 and Completing the Blue/Yellow Blocks.

Figure 8

Completing the Sashing Units

1. Sew C to each side of A; press seams toward C.

2. Sew C to D to make a C-D unit as shown in Figure 9; press seam toward D. Repeat to make four C-D units.

Figure 9

3. Join two C-D units to make a top unit, again referring to Figure 9; press seam in one direction. Repeat to make two top units.

4. Sew a top unit to the top and bottom of the A-C unit to complete one blue/orange sashing unit as shown in Figure 10. Repeat to make six blue/orange sashing units.

Blue/orange
Make 6

Figure 10

5. Repeat steps 1–4 with A, C and D pieces as shown in Figure 11 to complete six orange/blue sashing units.

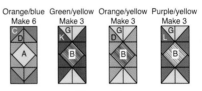

Orange/blue Green/yellow Orange/yellow Purple/yellow
Make 6   Make 3   Make 3   Make 3

Figure 11

6. Repeat steps 1–4 with B, K and G pieces to complete three green/yellow sashing units, again referring to Figure 11.

7. Repeat steps 1–4 with B, D and G pieces to complete three orange/yellow sashing units, again referring to Figure 11.

8. Repeat steps 1–4 with B, L and G to complete three purple/yellow sashing units, again referring to Figure 11.

Completing the Top

1. Join four Blue/Yellow blocks with three orange/blue sashing units to complete a yellow/orange row referring to Figure 12; repeat to make two yellow/orange rows. Press seams toward sashing units.

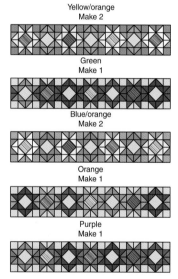

Yellow/orange
Make 2

Green
Make 1

Blue/orange
Make 2

Orange
Make 1

Purple
Make 1

Figure 12

2. Join four Yellow/Green blocks with three green/yellow sashing units to complete one green row, again referring to Figure 12; press seams toward the blocks.

3. Join four Yellow/Blue blocks with three blue/orange sashing units to complete one blue/orange row, again referring to Figure 12; repeat to make two blue/orange rows. Press seams toward sashing units.

4. Join four Yellow/Orange blocks with three orange/yellow sashing units to complete one orange row, again referring to Figure 12; press seams toward blocks.

5. Join four Yellow/Purple blocks with three purple/yellow sashing units to complete one purple row, again referring to Figure 12; press seams toward blocks.

6. Arrange and join the rows referring to the Placement Diagram for positioning; press seams in one direction.

7. Layer, quilt and bind referring to Finishing Your Quilt on page 173. ❖

Well-Connected Stars
Placement Diagram 66" x 84"

Starry Stripes

Lots of bright scraps can be used to make the hexagon shapes in this colorful quilt.

Design by **CONNIE KAUFFMAN**

PROJECT SPECIFICATIONS

Skill Level: Intermediate
Quilt Size: 49½" x 69½"

MATERIALS

- Bright-colored scraps in strips 1½"–3" wide for piecing
- Bright-colored 2"-wide scrap strips for borders
- 1¼ yards orange tonal
- 1½ yards yellow tonal
- Batting 56" x 76"
- Backing 56" x 76"
- All-purpose thread to match fabrics and yellow
- Quilting thread
- ½ yard 12"-wide fusible web
- Basic sewing tools and supplies

Cutting

1. Cut three 2¼" by fabric width E strips yellow tonal.

2. Cut two 2¼" x 32" F strips yellow tonal.

3. Cut six 2¼" by fabric width binding strips yellow tonal.

4. Prepare C and D templates using patterns given; cut as directed on each piece.

5. Cut six 6½" by fabric width K/L strips orange tonal.

6. Make copies of paper-piecing patterns as directed.

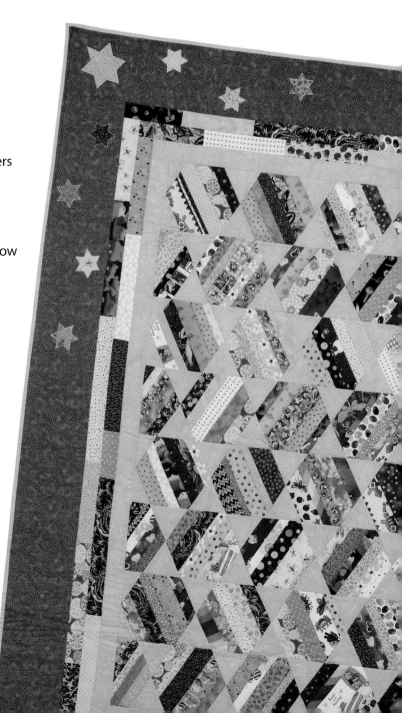

7. Trace star shapes onto the paper side of the fusible web as directed on pattern; cut out shapes, leaving a margin around each one.

8. Fuse shapes to the wrong side of fabric scraps as suggested; cut out shapes on traced lines. Remove paper backing.

Completing the Hexagon Units

1. Place one 1½"–3"-wide strip of bright fabric right side up across the unmarked side of an A paper-piecing pattern, using the lines on the other side to make sure the strip is at the right angle as shown in Figure 1; pin the strip in place.

Figure 1   Figure 2   Figure 3

2. Lay the next strip right side down on top of the pinned strip and sew along one edge as shown in Figure 2.

3. Press the strip to the right side as shown in Figure 3.

4. Continue sewing strips to both sides of the first strip until the paper hexagon is covered.

5. Trim excess fabric and paper on the solid outer line of the pattern to complete one hexagon.

6. Repeat steps 1–5 to complete to complete 28 A hexagons and eight B half-hexagons.

Completing the Top

1. Arrange four A hexagons with C, D and DR pieces to make an X row as shown in Figure 4. Join units and pieces as arranged; press seams toward C, D and DR pieces. Repeat to make four X rows.

2. Arrange three A hexagons and two B half-hexagons with C pieces to make a Y row, again referring to Figure 4. Join units and pieces as

arranged; press seams toward C. Repeat to make four Y rows.

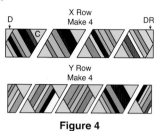

Figure 4

3. Arrange and join the rows to complete the pieced center referring to the Placement Diagram; press seams in one direction.

4. Join the E strips on short ends to make one long strip; press seams open. Subcut strip into two 48½" E strips.

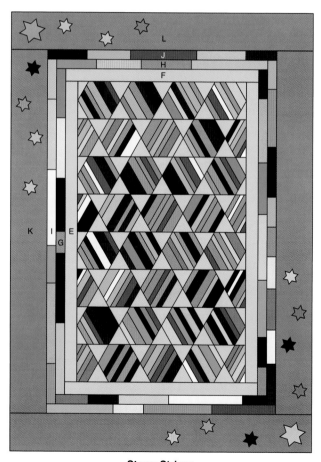

Starry Stripes
Placement Diagram 49½" x 69½"

5. Sew an E strip to opposite long sides and F strips to the top and bottom of the pieced center; press seams toward E and F strips.

6. Prepare a 375"-long strip of 2"-wide scraps and subcut into two strips each of the following lengths: 52" G, 35" H, 55" I and 38" J.

7. Sew the strips to the opposite long sides and then to the top and bottom of the pieced center in alphabetical order; press seams toward E and F strips.

8. Join the K/L strips on short ends to make one long strip; press seams open. Subcut strip into two 58" K strips and two 50" L strips.

9. Sew the K strips to opposite long sides and L strips to the top and bottom of the pieced center; press seams toward K and L strips.

10. Arrange and fuse star shapes on the K and L borders referring to the Placement Diagram for positioning.

11. Machine-stitch stars in place using yellow thread and a narrow blanket stitch to complete the top.

12. Layer, quilt and bind referring to Finishing Your Quilt on page 173. ✤

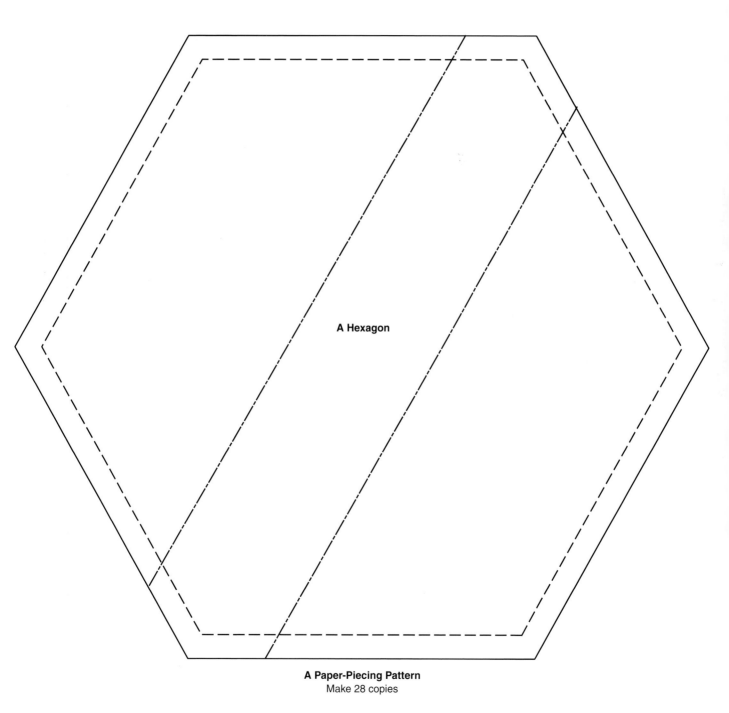

A Hexagon

A Paper-Piecing Pattern
Make 28 copies

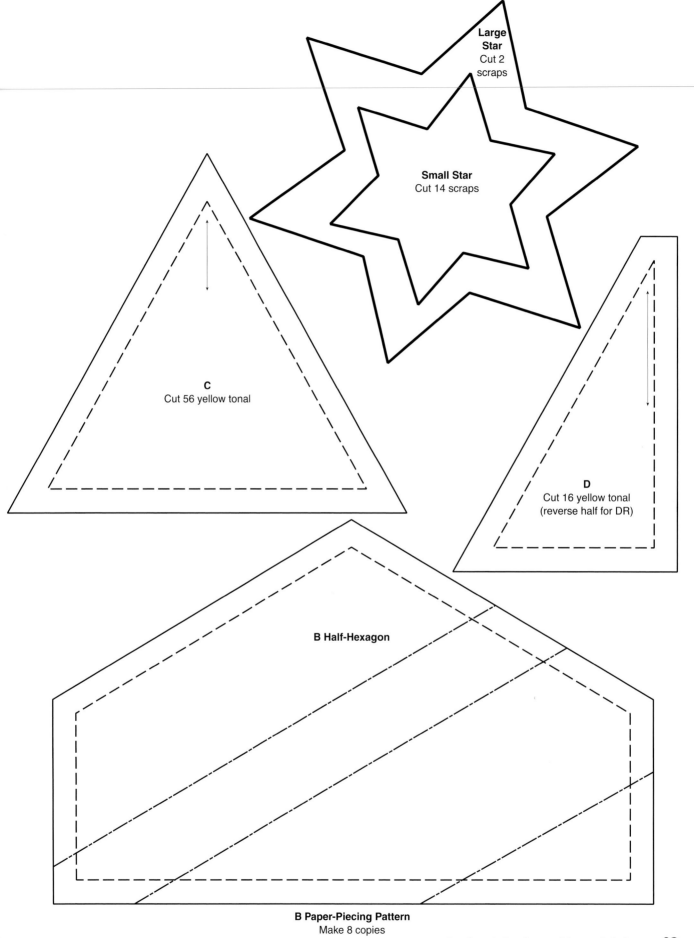

Large Star
Cut 2 scraps

Small Star
Cut 14 scraps

C
Cut 56 yellow tonal

D
Cut 16 yellow tonal
(reverse half for DR)

B Half-Hexagon

B Paper-Piecing Pattern
Make 8 copies

Floating Frames

Red, black and white make a dramatic statement in this easy-to-piece lap quilt.

Design by **SUE HARVEY & SANDY BOOBAR**

PROJECT SPECIFICATIONS

Skill Level: Beginner
Quillow Size: 63" x 72"
Block Size: 17" x 17"
Number of Blocks: 6

MATERIALS

- ¼ yard black print
- ¼ yard red print
- ⅝ yard red-and-black spaced floral
- ⅝ yard stripe
- ⅝ yard red-and-black circle print
- 1 yard black solid
- 1⅛ yards white tonal
- 1¼ yards red-and-black packed floral
- Batting 69" x 78"
- Backing 69" x 78"
- Neutral-color all-purpose thread
- Quilting thread
- Basic sewing tools and supplies

Cutting

1. Cut three 2" by fabric width strips black print; subcut strips into (12) 4" D and (12) 5½" G rectangles.

2. Cut three 2" by fabric width strips red print; subcut strips into (12) 4" F and (12) 5½" H rectangles.

3. Cut two 8½" by fabric width strips red-and-black spaced floral; subcut strips into six 8½" A squares.

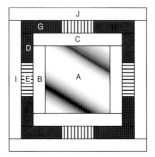

Floating Frames
17" x 17" Block
Make 6

4. Cut three 2" by fabric width strips stripe; subcut strips into (24) 4½" E rectangles.

5. Cut three 3½" by fabric width O strips stripe.

6. Cut two 2" by fabric width strips red-and-black circle print; subcut strips into three 17½" K strips.

7. Cut four 2" x 36" L strips red-and-black circle print.

8. Cut three 2" by fabric width M strips red-and-black circle print.

9. Cut eight 2" by fabric width N/P strips black solid.

10. Cut seven 2¼" by fabric width strips black solid for binding.

11. Cut (17) 2" by fabric width strips white tonal; subcut strips into 12 each 8½" B, 11½" C, 14½" I and 17½" J strips.

12. Cut six 6½" by fabric width Q/R strips red-and-black packed floral.

Completing the Floating Frames Blocks

1. Sew B to opposite sides and C to the top and bottom of the A squares; press seams toward the A squares.

2. Sew E between D and F as shown in Figure 1; press seams away from E. Repeat to make 12 D-E-F strips.

3. Sew E between G and H, again referring to Figure 1; press seams away from E. Repeat to make 12 E-G-H strips.

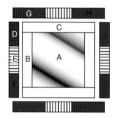

Figure 1 **Figure 2**

4. Sew D-E-F strips to opposite sides of the A-B-C units and E-G-H strips to the top and bottom as shown in Figure 2; press seams toward D-E-F and E-G-H.

5. Sew I to opposite sides and J to the top and bottom of the pieced units to complete the blocks; press seams away from I and J.

Completing the Top

1. Join two blocks with K to make a block row as shown in Figure 3; press seams toward K. Repeat to make three block rows.

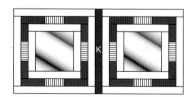

Figure 3

2. Join the block rows with the L strips, beginning and ending with an L strip; press seams toward L.

3. Join the M strips on the short ends to make a long strip; press seams to one side. Cut the strip into two 57½" M strips.

4. Repeat step 3 with the N/P strips. Cut the strip into four 57½" N strips and two 51" P strips.

5. Repeat step 3 with the O strips. Cut the strip into two 57½" O strips.

6. Repeat step 3 with the Q/R strips. Cut the strip into two 60½" Q strips and two 63½" R strips.

7. Sew the M strips to opposite long sides of the pieced center.

8. Sew an O strip between two N strips; press seams toward N. Repeat. Sew these strips to opposite long sides of the pieced center and the P strips to the top and bottom; press seams toward strips.

9. Sew the Q strips to opposite long sides and the R strips to the top and bottom of the pieced center to complete the top; press seams toward the strips.

10. Layer, quilt and bind referring to Finishing Your Quilt on page 173. ❖

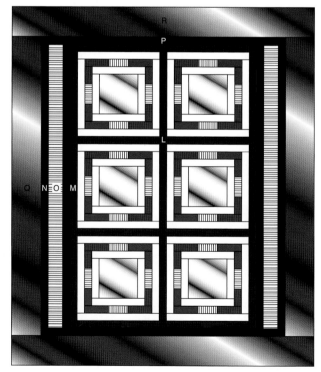

Floating Frames
Placement Diagram 63" x 72"

Patchwork Plus

Appliqué quilts are more popular today than ever. With fusible web, sewing machines that have special stitches and new techniques to try, not too many quilters are afraid to make an appliqué quilt. Adding a touch of appliqué just makes a quilt that much better.

Honey Bees Buzz

This quilt honors the honey bees that pollinate blossoms of flowers and many of the vegetables we eat.

Design by **CHRIS MALONE**

PROJECT SPECIFICATIONS

Skill Level: Intermediate
Quilt Size: 45¼" x 45¼"
Block Size: 12" x 12"
Number of Blocks: 9

MATERIALS

- ½ yard red tonal
- ½ yard orange print
- ⅝ yard multicolored stripe
- ¾ yard green tonal
- 1⅜ yards floral print
- Batting 52" x 52"
- Backing 52" x 52"
- All-purpose thread to match fabrics
- Quilting thread
- Basic sewing tools and supplies

Cutting

1. Cut two 6½" by fabric width strips floral print; subcut strips into nine 6½" A squares and four 4½" x 4½" G squares.

2. Trace appliquéd shape given to the wrong side of the floral print as directed; cut out shapes, adding a ¼" seam allowance all around when cutting for hand-appliqué.

3. Cut four 3½" by fabric width strips red tonal; subcut strips into eight 6½" B strips and eight 12½" C strips.

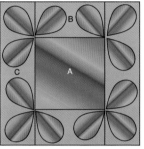

Orange Honey Bee
12" x 12" Block
Make 4

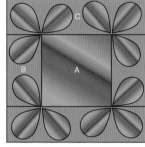

Green Honey Bee
12" x 12" Block
Make 1

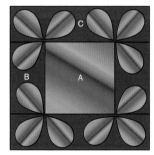

Red Honey Bee
12" x 12" Block
Make 4

4. Cut one 3½" by fabric width strip green tonal; subcut strip into two 6½" B strips and two 12½" C strips.

5. Cut two 1⅛" x 36½" D strip and two 1⅛" x 37¾" E strips green tonal.

6. Cut five 2¼" by fabric width strips green tonal for binding.

7. Cut four 3½" by fabric width strips orange print; subcut strips into eight 6½" B strips and eight 12½" C strips.

8. Cut four 4½" x 37¾" F strips multicolored stripe.

Completing the Blocks

1. Select two each red tonal B and C strips. Sew a B strip to opposite sides and C strips to the top and bottom of A; press seams toward B and C strips.

2. Turn under the seam allowance all around each bee shape; arrange and pin 12 bee shapes on the block with ends pointing toward the center and corners referring to Figure 1. Hand- or machine-stitch shapes in place.

Figure 1

3. Repeat steps 1 and 2 to make four each Red Honey Bee and Orange Honey Bee blocks and one Green Honey Bee block referring to the block drawings.

Completing the Top

1. Sew an Orange Honey Bee block between two Red Honey Bee blocks to make a row; repeat to make two rows.

2. Sew a Green Honey Bee block between two Orange Honey Bee blocks to make a row.

3. Sew the orange/green row between the red/orange rows to complete the pieced center.

4. Sew D strips to top and bottom of the pieced center, and E strips to opposite sides; press seams toward D and E strips.

5. Sew an F strip to opposite sides of the pieced center; press seams toward F strips.

6. Sew a G square to each end of each remaining F strip; press seams toward F. Sew the F-G strips to the top and bottom of the pieced center to complete the top; press seams toward the F-G strips.

7. Layer, quilt and bind referring to Finishing Your Quilt on page 173. ❖

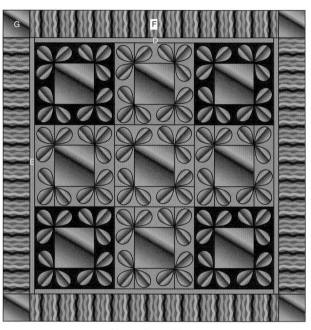

Honey Bees Buzz
Placement Diagram 45¼" x 45¼"

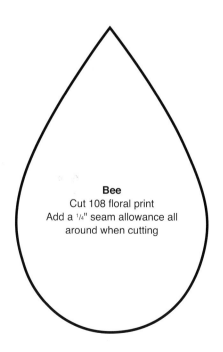

Bee
Cut 108 floral print
Add a ¼" seam allowance all
around when cutting

Crazy-Patch Roses

When you combine 3-D leaves with simple pieced blocks,
a whole new design appears.

Design by **CHRIS MALONE**

PROJECT NOTE

With crazy-patchwork, there are no set sizes to cut or set seam placements. The technique used to make the Rose blocks in this project is a sew-and-flip method using the muslin squares as a foundation for the block. Use a slightly longer-than-normal stitch length, and do not backstitch at the end of the seams.

PROJECT SPECIFICATIONS

Skill Level: Intermediate
Quilt Size: 45" x 45"
Block Size: 9" x 9"
Number of Blocks: 25

MATERIALS

- Scrap gold print
- ½ yard green print or tonal for leaf facings
- ½ yard green print for binding
- ¾ yard muslin
- 1 yard total assorted medium to dark green prints and tonals for leaves
- 1 yard total assorted scraps medium to dark rose prints and tonals for rose blocks
- 1⅝ yards total assorted light to medium tan prints and tonals for Patchwork A and B blocks
- Batting 51" x 51"
- Backing 51" x 51"
- All-purpose thread to match fabrics
- Quilting thread
- Variegated (or solid) rose pearl cotton, size 5
- Basic sewing tools and supplies

Cutting

1. Prepare templates for C and leaf using patterns given; cut C as directed.

2. Cut (96) 3½" x 3½" A squares from the assorted light to medium tans.

3. Cut (56) 3½" x 5" B rectangles from the assorted light to medium tans.

4. Cut two 10½" by fabric width strips muslin; subcut strips into five 10½" base squares.

5. Cut about (90) 7½"-long strips, 1"–1¾" wide from the medium to dark greens for leaf piecing.

6. Cut five 2¼" by fabric width strips green print for binding.

Completing the Patchwork Blocks

1. To piece one Patchwork A block, arrange six A squares with two B rectangles in three horizontal rows as shown in Figure 1.

Figure 1

2. Join the short seams in each row; press seams in one direction.

3. Join the rows as arranged to complete one Patchwork A block; press seams in one direction.

4. Repeat steps 1–3 to complete 12 Patchwork A blocks.

5. To piece one Patchwork B block, arrange three A squares with four B rectangles in three horizontal rows as shown in Figure 2.

Figure 2

6. Join the short seams in each row; press seams in one direction.

7. Join the rows as arranged to complete one Patchwork B block; press seams in one direction.

8. Repeat steps 5–7 to complete eight Patchwork B blocks.

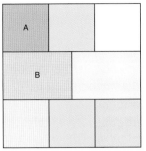

Patchwork A
9" x 9" Block
Make 12

Patchwork B
9" x 9" Block
Make 8

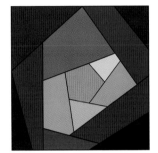

Rose
9" x 9" Block
Make 5

Completing the Rose Blocks

1. To complete one Rose block, pin a C piece right side up and slightly off-center on one muslin base as shown in Figure 3.

Figure 3　　　　　**Figure 4**

2. Place a strip about 2½"-wide of medium-value rose over one side of C with right sides together; sew a ¼" seam through all three layers as shown in Figure 4.

3. Flip the added strip over so the right side is up and press as shown in Figure 5.

Figure 5

4. Select a different medium-rose strip and attach it to the adjacent side (moving clockwise) of C, make the strip long enough to cover the edge of the first strip. Sew a ¼" seam and trim the section of the first piece that you just stitched over to ¼" as shown in Figure 6. ***Note:*** *You may have to remove a few stitches to release the fabric to trim.*

Figure 6

5. Continue piecing clockwise, adding a strip of medium-rose fabric to each side of the C center.

6. Begin the second round in the same manner, using the darker rose prints and wider (about 3") strips varying the angles to make each rose petal different.

7. For the third round, continue using the darker prints until the foundation square is covered. ***Note:*** *You will probably only need to add four pieces, one for each corner.*

8. Press the square well and trim it to 9½" x 9½". Machine-baste all around ³⁄₁₆" from the edge.

9. Using 1 strand of rose pearl cotton, make six or seven straight stitches in the flower center, radiating out from the center point. ***Note:*** *The stitches should be a little irregular in length and placement.*

10. Make a French knot at each stitch end and in the center as shown in Figure 7.

Figure 7

11. Repeat steps 1–10 to complete five Rose blocks.

Completing the Leaves

1. Using the assorted green fabrics of varying widths, join enough strips together along the 7½" side to make a 7½" x 7½" square; press seams open. ***Note:*** *If your strips go beyond the 7½" size, it is not a problem, as they will be trimmed.* Repeat to make 12 strip-pieced squares.

2. Trim each piece to 7¼" x 7¼" square. Divide the squares into two groups of six each.

3. Cut each block of one group on the diagonal from the upper left corner to the lower right corner as shown in Figure 8.

Figure 8

4. Cut the remaining blocks on the diagonal from the lower left corner to the upper right corner as shown in Figure 9. ***Note:*** *Be sure you have the strips going in the same direction before cutting.*

Figure 9

5. Take one triangle from each group and sew them together along the cut diagonal edge as shown in Figure 10; press seam open. Repeat to make a total of 12 pieced squares.

Figure 10

6. Trace the leaf template 12 times onto the wrong side of the green facing fabric, leaving about a 1" margin between the shapes; transfer the dots from the pattern to the fabric.

7. Cut the leaves apart and pin a leaf facing to a pieced leaf square with right sides together and with dots at the tip and base aligned with a diagonal seam as shown in Figure 11.

Figure 11

8. Stitch directly on the pattern line, leaving open at the bottom edge; cut out ⅛" from stitched seam, trim the tip and turn right side out. Press. Repeat to make a total of 12 leaves.

Completing the Top

1. Arrange the Patchwork A and B blocks, and the Rose blocks in five rows of five blocks each referring to the Placement Diagram for positioning of blocks. Note that the Patchwork A and B blocks are all vertical and there is one Rose block in each row.

2. Again referring to the Placement Diagram, arrange the leaves around the rose blocks. When satisfied with placement, pick up each Patchwork A or B block with a leaf or two leaves.

3. Center and machine-baste the bottom edge of the leaf or leaves onto the block ³⁄₁₆" from the edge as shown in Figure 12. When stitching is complete, return the blocks to the arrangement.

Figure 12

4. Join the blocks together in rows as arranged; press each seam between a Rose block and a leaf block toward the Rose block so the leaf will fall naturally away from the rose to complete the top.

Completing the Quilt

1. Sandwich the batting between the completed top and prepared backing; pin or baste layers together to hold.

2. Quilt as desired by hand or machine; remove pins or basting. Trim excess backing and batting even with quilt top. ***Note:*** *The sample was machine-quilted using a walking foot with wavy lines down each vertical strip to suggest a trellis. The Rose blocks have stitching in the ditch around the center, around the first row of petals and around the Rose block. The leaves are stitched about 4" down the center, leaving the tips free.*

3. Join binding strips on short ends with diagonal seams to make one long strip; trim seams to ¼" and press seams open. Fold the strip in half along length with wrong sides together; press.

4. Sew binding to the right side of the quilt edges, overlapping ends. Fold binding to the back side and stitch in place to finish. ✤

Crazy Patch Roses
Placement Diagram 45" x 45"

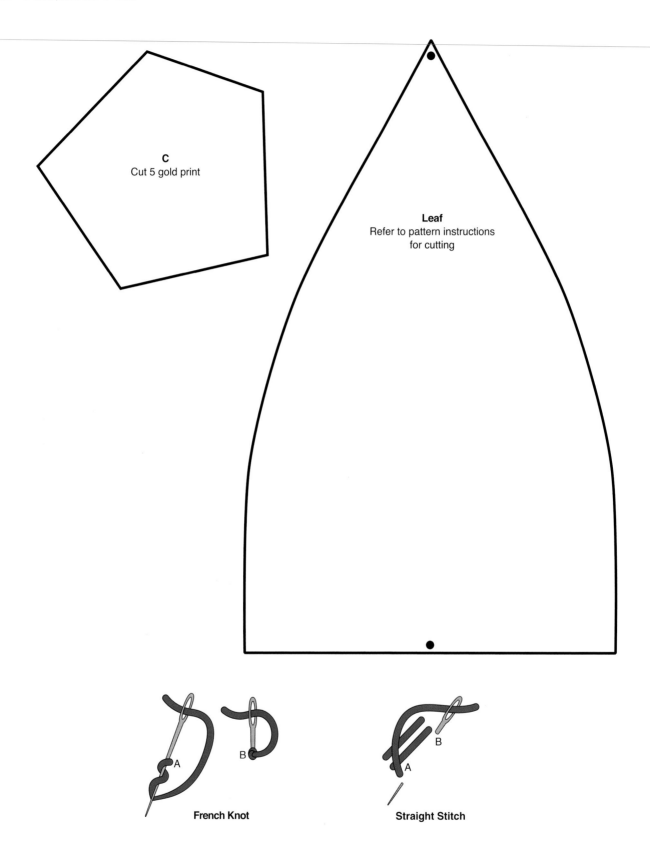

C
Cut 5 gold print

Leaf
Refer to pattern instructions
for cutting

A

B

French Knot

B

A

Straight Stitch

Diamonds in the Garden

Because the colors are different in every block, this quilt is best stitched in units.

Design by **BRENDA CONNELLY & BARB MILLER FROM BRENDABARB DESIGNS**

PROJECT SPECIFICATIONS

Skill Level: Advanced
Quilt Size: 44" x 68"
Block Size: 12" x 12"
Number of Blocks: 7

MATERIALS

- ⅛ yard each 5–7 color sets in blue, purple, yellow, pink and green (light-medium, medium and dark-medium) with a mixture of batiks, mottleds or solids for flower blocks
- ½ yard dark tan mottled
- ⅝ yard each light tan, and medium and dark brown mottleds
- ¾ yard cream tonal
- 1⅛ yards black solid
- Batting 50" x 74"
- Backing 50" x 74"
- All-purpose thread to match fabrics
- Quilting thread
- ¼ yard 18"-wide fusible web
- Light box
- Permanent fabric pen
- Basic sewing tools and supplies

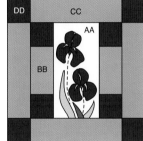

Iris
12" x 12" Block
Make 7 in various colors

Cutting

1. Cut one 4½" by fabric width strip cream tonal; subcut strip into nine 4½" A squares.

2. Cut one 2½" by fabric width strip cream tonal; subcut strip into (14) 2½" squares.

3. Cut one 4½" by fabric width strip cream tonal; subcut strip into three 8½" rectangles.

4. Cut one 9½" by fabric width strip cream tonal; subcut strip into seven 5½" AA rectangles.

5. Cut two same-fabric 2½" x 4½" BB rectangles from light-medium flower-block fabric; repeat to cut seven sets of two BB rectangles.

6. Cut three 4½" by fabric width strips light tan; subcut strips into (22) 4½" B squares.

7. Cut one 4½" by fabric width strip light tan; subcut strip into two 8½" rectangles and four 2½" x 2½" squares.

8. Cut four same-fabric 2½" x 8½" CC rectangles from a medium flower-block fabric; repeat to cut seven sets of four CC rectangles.

9. Cut two 4½" by fabric width strips dark tan; subcut strips into (11) 4½" C squares and three 8½" rectangles.

10. Cut one 2½" by fabric width strip dark tan; subcut strip into (14) 2½" squares.

11. Cut three 4½" by fabric width strips medium brown; subcut strips into (22) 4½" D squares.

12. Cut one 2½" by fabric width strip medium brown; subcut strip into six 2½" squares.

13. Cut eight same-fabric 2½" DD squares from a dark-medium flower-block fabric; repeat to cut seven sets of eight DD squares.

14. Cut three 4½" by fabric width strips dark brown; subcut strips into (26) 4½" E squares.

15. Cut one 2½" by fabric width strips dark brown; subcut strips into (10) 2½" squares.

16. Cut four 4½" by fabric width strips black solid; subcut strips into (28) 4½" F squares and (12) 2½" W rectangles.

17. Cut six 2¼" by fabric width strips black solid for binding.

Completing Unit 1

1. To complete one Unit 1, draw a diagonal line on a 2½" square and place on a 4½" square right side down as shown in Figure 1.

Figure 1

2. Stitch on the marked line on the smaller square, trim seam to ¼", fold the smaller square to the right side and press as shown in Figure 1 to complete a Unit 1.

Completing Unit 2

1. Refer to steps 1 and 2 for Unit 1.

2. Repeat these steps with a second 2½" square on the adjacent corner of the 4½" square to complete Unit 2 as shown in Figure 2.

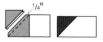

Figure 2

Completing Unit 3

1. Mark a diagonal line on the wrong side of two 4½" F squares.

2. Place one square on one end of a 4½" x 8½" rectangle and stitch on the marked line as shown in Figure 3; trim seam to ¼" and press the square to the right side, again referring to Figure 3.

Figure 3

3. Repeat step 2 on the opposite end of the rectangle to complete a Unit 3 as shown in Figure 4.

Figure 4

Construct the Following Using Unit 1 Instructions

Note: *Refer to Figure 5 for all steps in this section.*

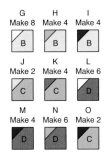

Figure 5

1. Make eight units using a 4½" B square and a 2½" cream tonal square; label G.

2. Make four units using a 4½" B square and a 2½" dark tan square; label H.

3. Make four units using a 4½" B square and a 2½" dark brown square; label I.

4. Make two units using a 4½" C square and a 2½" light tan square; label J.

5. Make four units using a 4½" C square and a 2½" medium brown square; label K.

6. Make six units using a 4½" D square and a 2½" cream tonal square; label L.

7. Make four units using a 4½" D square and a 2½" dark brown square; label M.

8. Make six units using a 4½" D square and a 2½" dark tan square; label N.

9. Make two units using a 4½" C square and a 2½" dark brown square; label O.

Construct the Following Using Unit 2 Instructions

Note: *Refer to Figure 6 for all steps in this section.*

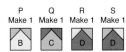

Figure 6

1. Make one unit using a 4½" B square and two 2½" dark tan squares; label P.

2. Make one unit using a 4½" C square and two 2½" medium brown squares; label Q.

3. Make one unit using a 4½" D square and a 2½" light tan square first and a 2½" dark tan square second; label R.

4. Make one unit using a 4½" D square, a 2½" dark tan square first and a 2½" light tan square second; label S.

Completing the Odd-Numbered Blocks

1. Lay out units and squares in three rows of three units/squares each to complete block 1 as shown in Figure 7; press seams in one direction.

Figure 7

2. Repeat step 1 to complete blocks 3, 5, 7, 9, 11, 13 and 15 as shown in Figure 8. Press seams in center rows opposite those in the top and bottom rows in each block.

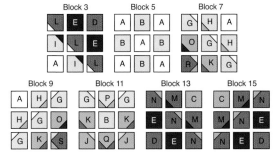

Figure 8

Completing the Iris Blocks

1. Place the iris pattern of your choice right side down on a light box; lay the fusible web, paper side down, on top of the pattern. ***Note:*** *To vary the arrangement, place the pattern right side up.*

2. Trace the pieces in numerical order with a soft lead pencil, leaving at least ¼" between the pieces. Extend the part of any piece that lies under a larger-numbered piece at least ⅛". Number each piece as you trace.

3. Lay an AA rectangle right side up on the iris pattern; trace the outline of each iris onto AA using a fabric pen; let dry and then heat-set. Repeat with all AA rectangles.

4. Cut out the fusible-web pieces at least ¼" beyond the lines; iron the fusible web pieces paper side up to the wrong side of fabrics as directed on each piece for color suggestions. Remove paper.

5. Place an AA rectangle on top of the paper pattern and lay iris pieces right side up on top in numerical order referring to pattern and marked outlines. When satisfied with positioning, iron pieces in place.

6. Trim the rectangle with appliqué to 4½" x 8½".

7. Sew a DD square to opposite ends of a BB rectangle as shown in Figure 9; press seams toward DD. Repeat to make two BB-DD units.

Figure 9

Figure 10

8. Sew a BB-DD unit to opposite sides of the iris rectangle as shown in Figure 10; press seams toward BB-DD.

9. Sew a DD square to each end of a CC rectangle; press seams toward CC. Repeat to make two CC-DD units.

10. Sew a CC rectangle to the BB-DD sides of the pieced unit and the CC-DD units to the top and bottom of the pieced unit as shown in Figure 11 to complete one Iris block.

Figure 11

11. Repeat steps 5–8 to complete seven different-colored Iris blocks referring to the Placement Diagram for color configurations.

Construct the Following Using Unit 3 Instructions

Note: *Refer to Figure 12 for all steps in this section.*

Figure 12

1. Make three units using a 4½" x 8½" cream tonal rectangle and two 4½" F squares; label T.

2. Make two units using a 4½" x 8½" light tan rectangle and two 4½" F squares; label U.

3. Make three units using a 4½" x 8½" dark tan rectangle and two 4½" F squares; label V.

Completing the Top

1. Arrange and join the odd-numbered and Iris blocks in five rows of three blocks each referring to Figure 13 for numerical placement; press odd-numbered rows to the right and even-numbered rows to the left.

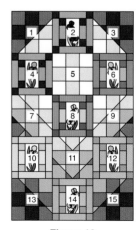

Figure 13

2. Join two F and four E squares with one T unit and two W rectangles to make the top border as shown in Figure 14; press seams away from T. Repeat to make the bottom border using a V unit instead of the T unit.

Figure 14

3. Sew the strips to the top and bottom of the pieced center referring to the Placement Diagram for positioning; press seams toward borders.

4. Join four F and five E squares, one each T, U and V units, and four W rectangles to make the right-side border as shown in Figure 15; press seams away from T, U and V units. Repeat to make the left-side border.

Figure 15

5. Sew the strips to the right and left sides of the pieced center referring to the Placement Diagram for positioning; press seams toward strips to complete the pieced top.

6. Layer, quilt and bind referring to Finishing Your Quilt on page 173. ❖

Diamonds in the Garden
Placement Diagram 44" x 68"

Iris Motif 1
Make 1 each blue & pink
Reverse & make 1 each purple & yellow
Refer to project photo for color
placement

Iris Motif 2
Make 1 purple
Reverse & make 1 each yellow & pink
Refer to project photo for color
placement

Patchwork Flowers

Bright flowers blossom all year long in this colorful quilt.

Design by **CHRIS MALONE**

PROJECT SPECIFICATIONS

Skill Level: Intermediate
Quilt Size: 56" x 40"
Block Size: 8" x 8"
Number of Blocks: 35

MATERIALS

- 17 (6" x 6") squares assorted red, blue and yellow prints
- ¾ yards total green prints or 6–8 fat eighths
- 2 yards total light–medium tan tonals or 8 assorted fat quarters
- Batting 60" x 46"
- Backing 60" x 46"
- Neutral-color all-purpose thread
- Quilting thread
- Basic sewing tools and supplies

Cutting

1. From each of the 6" x 6" squares, cut one 2½" x 2½" A square and three 3" x 3" B squares. Pin the same-fabric pieces together to make a total of 17 sets.

2. Cut two 3" x 3" matching C squares green prints to total 34 sets of green C squares.

3. Cut one 4½" x 4½" D square, three 3" x 3" F squares and three 2½" x 2½" E squares from one tan tonal to make one block set; repeat to make 17 block sets.

4. Cut (54) 4½" x 4½" H squares total tan tonals.

5. Cut (72) 2½" x 2½" G squares total tan tonals.

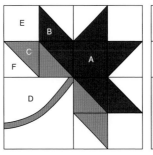

Flower
8" x 8" Block
Make 17

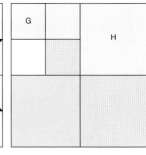

Four-Patch
8" x 8" Block
Make 18

6. Cut one 1½" x 6" green bias strip to match each set of C squares.

7. Prepare a template for leaf pattern; cut two leaves to match each set of C squares, adding ¼" all around for seam allowance.

8. Cut 2¼"-wide strips assorted green prints to total 220" for binding.

Completing the Flower Blocks

Note: *Use a ¼" seam allowance throughout. Positioning of flower blocks varies a little to add interest. About half the stems curve in opposite directions and the leaves are placed to vary slightly from flower to flower.*

1. To complete one Flower block, select one matching set each A and B, one matching set C and bias strip, and one matching set of D, E and F squares.

2. Mark a diagonal line from corner to corner on the wrong side of each F square and one C square.

3. With right sides together, place two of the F squares with the B squares and the remaining F square with an unmarked C square. Place remaining B square with the marked C square.

4. Stitch ¼" from each side of the drawn line on each layered set as shown in Figure 1; cut apart on drawn line, again referring to Figure 1.

Figure 1

5. Open and press seams toward B or C.

6. Trim each unit to 2½" x 2½" square, keeping the diagonal seam centered.

7. Sew a B-C unit to a B-F unit to make a row as shown in Figure 2; press seam toward B-F.

8. Sew a C-F unit to E to make a row, again referring to Figure 2; press seam toward E.

Figure 2

9. Join the two rows to complete one block quarter; press seam toward the E side.

10. Sew a B-C unit to a C-F unit to make a row as shown in Figure 3; press seam toward the B-C unit.

11. Sew a B-F unit to E to make a row, again referring to Figure 3; press seam toward E.

12. Join the rows to make a second block quarter, again referring to Figure 3; press seam toward the E side.

Figure 3   **Figure 4**

13. Sew B-F to A to make a row as shown in Figure 4; press seam toward A.

14. Sew B-F to E to make a row, again referring to Figure 4; press seam toward E.

15. Join the rows to complete a third block quarter, again referring to Figure 4; press seam toward the A side.

16. To prepare stem for appliqué, fold the bias strip in half along length with wrong sides together; sew along the long raw edge. Trim the seam to a scant ⅛" and press with seam on the center back as shown in Figure 5.

Figure 5

17. Referring to the block drawing and Placement Diagram for positioning, pin the bias stem to a D square, placing stem at one corner and gently curving it on the diagonal ending 1⅛" in from the opposite corner as shown in Figure 6. Trim off any excess.

Figure 6

18. Appliqué the stem in place by hand or machine.

19. Arrange the block quarters as shown in Figure 7; join the block quarters in rows and then join the rows to complete one Flower block, pressing seams in rows in opposite direction and block seam in one direction.

Figure 7

20. Repeat steps 1–19 to complete 17 Flower blocks.

Completing the Four-Patch Blocks

1. Select four G squares and three H squares.

2. Join two G squares to make a row; press seam in one direction. Repeat to make two rows. Join the rows to make a Four-Patch unit; press seam in one direction.

3. Sew the Four-Patch unit to H as shown in Figure 8; press seam toward H.

Figure 8

4. Join two H squares to make a row; press seam in one direction.

5. Join the H row with the Four-Patch row to complete one Four-Patch block referring to the block drawing; press seam in one direction.

6. Repeat steps 1–5 to complete 18 Four-Patch blocks.

Completing the Top

1. Join two Flower blocks with three Four-Patch blocks to make an X row referring to the Placement Diagram for positioning; press seams toward Four-Patch blocks. Repeat to make four X rows. ***Note:*** *The Flower blocks and the Four-Patch blocks are turned in different ways on each row.*

2. Join two Four-Patch blocks with three Flower blocks to make a Y row referring to the Placement Diagram for positioning; press seams toward Four-Patch blocks. Repeat to make three Y rows.

3. Join the X and Y rows referring to the Placement Diagram for positioning; press seams in one direction.

4. Pin two matching leaf shapes on each stem piece referring to the Placement Diagram for positioning; turn under seam allowance all around and hand-stitch in place to complete the top.

5. Layer, quilt and bind referring to Finishing Your Quilt on page 173. ✤

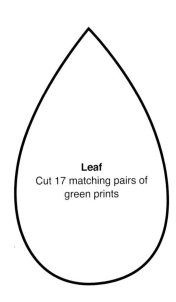

Leaf
Cut 17 matching pairs of green prints

Patchwork Flowers
Placement Diagram 40" x 56"

Summer Charm

Add a touch of summer using a charm-square pack and some appliqué.

Design by **CHRIS MALONE**

PROJECT SPECIFICATIONS

Skill Level: Intermediate
Quilt Size: 40½" x 40½"

MATERIALS

- 2 charm packs or 66 (5" x 5") assorted squares for A
- Assorted scraps for appliqué
- ¼ yard red tonal
- ½ yard coordinating floral
- ⅞ yard white tonal
- Batting 47" x 47"
- Backing 47" x 47"
- All-purpose thread to match fabrics
- Quilting thread
- ¼ yard lightweight nonwoven interfacing
- 4½ yards green medium rickrack
- 2 yards black baby rickrack
- 30" x 4" strip of paper
- Air-soluble marking pen
- 4 (¾") white buttons
- 12 (⁹⁄₁₆") white buttons
- Basic sewing tools and supplies

Cutting

1. Cut two 1¼" x 28½" B strips and two 1¼" x 30" C strips red tonal.

2. Cut four 6" x 30" D strips white tonal.

3. Cut five 2¼" by fabric width strips coordinating floral for binding.

Completing the Stitched Units

1. Mark a diagonal line from corner to corner on the wrong side of 33 A squares.

2. Pair up a marked A square with an unmarked A square and place right sides together.

3. Stitch ¼" on each side of the marked line as shown in Figure 1; cut apart on the marked line to make two A units, again referring to Figure 1.

Figure 1

4. Repeat steps 2 and 3 with all marked A squares to complete 66 A units; set aside one unit for another project.

5. Join four A units as shown in Figure 2; press seams in rows in opposite directions and then in one direction. Trim the stitched unit to 6" x 6" for corner units, keeping the center of the stitched unit as the center of the trimmed unit. Repeat to make four corner units.

Figure 2

6. Trim the remaining A units to 4½" x 4½".

Completing the Top

1. Arrange and join seven A units to make a row as shown in Figure 3; press seams in one direction.

Repeat to make seven rows, press seams in three rows in one direction and in four rows in the opposite direction.

Figure 3

2. Join the rows with seams in opposite directions; press seams in one direction to complete the pieced center.

3. Sew a B strip to opposite sides and C strips to the top and bottom of the pieced center; press seams toward B and C strips.

4. To prepare the curved vine pattern, fold the paper strip in half crosswise and in half again. Place the pattern given on top and mark the curve; cut out on the marked line.

5. Unfold paper pattern and place on a D strip with the straight edge of the pattern aligned with a long edge of the D strip; draw the curve on the fabric with the air-soluble marking pen. Repeat on each D strip.

6. Place the green rickrack over the line on each D strip, extending the rickrack into the seam allowance; pin to secure. Trim off excess. Sew in place by hand or machine.

7. Trace 12 flowers, 28 leaves and four dragonfly bodies on the wrong side of the remaining charm pack squares or assorted scraps, leaving at least a ¼" space between shapes. ***Note:*** *You can also use leftovers from the red tonal and coordinating floral.*

8. Pin the marked squares to the lightweight interfacing, marked side up, and sew all around on the marked lines with a short stitch.

9. Cut out each shape ⅛" from the stitching and clip curves and leaf tips. Cut a slash in the interfacing side only; turn the shapes right side out through the slash; press well.

10. Referring to the project photo and the Placement Diagram for positioning, arrange and pin three flowers, seven leaves and one dragonfly body to each D strip.

11. To make dragonfly wings, cut (16) 4"-long pieces of black baby rickrack. Use the pattern given to draw the wing placement with the air-soluble marking pen. Lift the upper body and shape each piece of rickrack to fit the wing patterns; pin and hand-stitch in place to secure.

12. Hand- or machine-appliqué each shape in place.

13. Use 2 strands black embroidery floss to embroider French knots on each dragonfly for eyes referring to Figure 4 and the pattern for placement.

Figure 4

14. Sew an appliquéd D strip to opposite sides of the pieced center; press seams away from D strips.

15. Sew a corner unit to each end of each remaining appliquéd D strip; sew these strips to the top and bottom of the pieced center to complete the top. Press seams away from D strips.

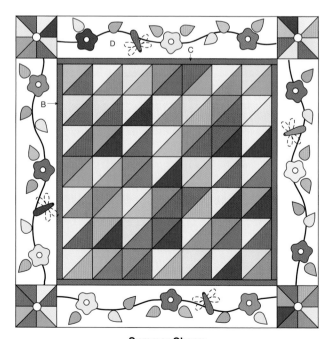

Summer Charm
Placement Diagram 40½" x 40½"

16. Layer, quilt and bind referring to Finishing Your Quilt on page 173.

17. Sew a ¾" button to each corner unit and a ⁹⁄₁₆" button to each flower center to finish. ❖

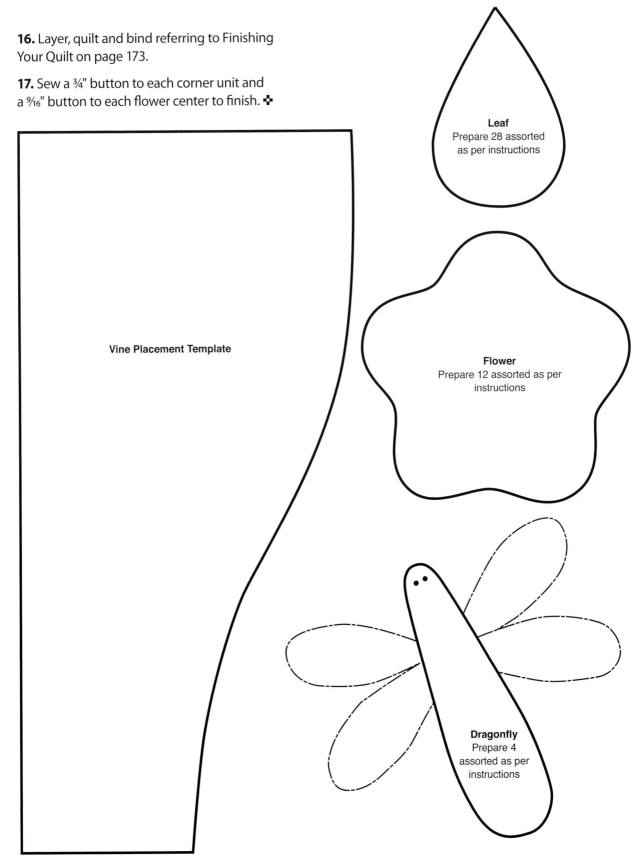

Vine Placement Template

Leaf
Prepare 28 assorted as per instructions

Flower
Prepare 12 assorted as per instructions

Dragonfly
Prepare 4 assorted as per instructions

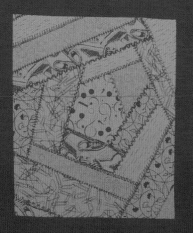

The New Classic

Classic quilts today are far from boring or even traditional. They may start with a traditional block or quilt setting, but by adding a few twists and turns, these quilts will attract anyone's eye. You might like the classic block, but you'll love the new look we've given to it.

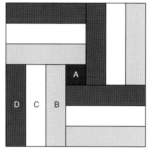

Interwoven Melodies

Use black, gray and white music prints to create the interwoven blocks in this melodious quilt.

Design by **CONNIE KAUFFMAN**

PROJECT SPECIFICATIONS

Skill Level: Intermediate
Quilt Size: 54" x 72"
Block Size: 14" x 14"
Number of Blocks: 12

MATERIALS

Note: *Fabric is 43" usable width.*
- ⅔ yard red solid
- 1 yard white music print
- 1 yard gray music print
- 1 yard black music print
- 1¼ yards black solid
- Batting 60" x 80"
- Backing 60" x 80"
- All-purpose thread to match fabrics
- Red and white quilting thread
- Basic sewing tools and supplies

Cutting

1. Cut one 2½" by fabric width strip red solid; subcut strip into (12) 2½" A squares.

2. Cut seven 2¼" by fabric width strips red solid for binding.

3. Cut (11) 2½" by fabric width strips each gray music print (B), white music print (C) and black music print (D).

4. Cut six 6½" by fabric width E/F strips black solid.

Interwoven Melodies
14" x 14" Block
Make 12

Completing the Blocks

1. Sew a B strip to a C strip to a D strip with right sides together along length to make a B-C-D strip set; press seams in one direction. Repeat to make 11 B-C-D strip sets.

2. Subcut the B-C-D strip sets into (50) 8½" units, two 2½" units and two 4½" units as shown in Figure 1.

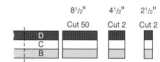

Figure 1

3. To complete one Interwoven Melodies block, select four 8½" units and one A square.

4. Sew A to one 8½" unit, stopping stitching 1½" from end as shown in Figure 2; press seam away from A.

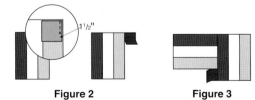

Figure 2   **Figure 3**

5. Add a second 8½" unit to the stitched unit as shown in Figure 3; press seam away from A.

6. Continue to add units all around A as shown in Figure 4; press seams away from A.

Figure 4   **Figure 5**

7. After stitching the last unit to A, complete the partial seam as shown in Figure 5 to complete one block; press seam away from A.

8. Repeat steps 3–7 to complete 12 Interwoven Melodies blocks.

Completing the Top

1. Join four Interwoven Melodies blocks to make a row as shown in Figure 6; repeat to make three rows. Press seams in one row in one direction and in the remaining two rows in the opposite direction.

Figure 6

2. Select one of the two remaining B-C-D units; remove the gray B strip as shown in Figure 7.

3. Select the remaining B-C-D unit; remove the black D strip, again referring to Figure 7.

Figure 7

4. Sew a 2½" unit to the end of the black D strip and a 4½" unit to the end of the C-D unit as shown in Figure 8; press seams in one direction.

Figure 8

5. Sew a 4½" unit to the end of the B-C unit and a 2½" unit to the end of the gray B strip as shown in Figure 9; press seams in one direction.

Figure 9

6. Sew the pieced units to the end of the rows referring to Figure 10 for placement; press seams in the same direction as those in the row being stitched.

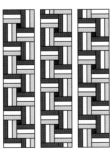

Figure 10

7. Join the rows as arranged; press seams in one direction.

8. Join the E/F strips on short ends to make one long strip; press seams open. Subcut strip into two 60½" E strips and two 54½" F strips.

9. Sew E strips to opposite long sides and F strips to the top and bottom of the pieced center; press seams toward E and F strips to complete the pieced top.

10. Layer, quilt and bind referring to Finishing Your Quilt on page 173. ***Note:*** *The project shown was quilted in a music bar pattern with note shapes inserted as in written music.* ✤

Interwoven Melodies
Placement Diagram 54" x 72"

Polka Dots & Paisleys

Squares and triangles combine in blocks stitched in vertical rows to create the design in this fun quilt.

Design by JILL REBER

PROJECT SPECIFICATIONS

Skill Level: Beginner
Quilt Size: 42" x 54"
Block Size: 6" x 6"
Number of Blocks: 28

MATERIALS

Note: *Fabric is 43" usable width.*
- ½ yard brown/pink dot
- ½ yard pink tonal
- ½ yard pink/brown dot
- ⅝ yard pink print
- ¾ yard brown paisley
- ⅞ yard white tonal
- Batting 48" x 60"
- Backing 48" x 60"
- Neutral-color all-purpose thread
- Quilting thread
- Basic sewing tools and supplies

Cutting

1. Cut three 3⅞" by fabric width strips pink tonal; subcut strips into (28) 3⅞" squares. Cut each square in half on one diagonal to make 56 A triangles.

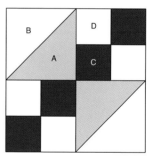

Jacob's Ladder
6" x 6" Block
Make 28

2. Cut six 2" by fabric width C strips brown/pink dot.

3. Cut three 3⅞" by fabric width strips white tonal; subcut strips into (28) 3⅞" squares. Cut each square in half on one diagonal to make 56 B triangles.

4. Cut six 2" by fabric width D strips white tonal.

5. Cut five 2½" x 42½" E strips pink print.

6. Cut two 2½" x 34½" F strips pink print.

7. Cut three 4½" by fabric width G strips brown paisley.

8. Cut two 4½" x 42½" H strips brown paisley.

9. Cut five 2¼" by fabric width strips pink/brown dot for binding.

Completing the Blocks

Note: *Use a ¼" seam allowance throughout.*

1. Sew a C strip to a D strip with right sides together along length; press seam toward C. Repeat to make six C-D strip sets.

2. Subcut the C-D strip sets into (112) 2" C-D units as shown in Figure 1.

Figure 1   **Figure 2**

3. To complete one Jacob's Ladder block, sew A to B to complete an A-B unit as shown in Figure 2;

press seam toward A. Repeat to complete two A-B units.

4. Join two C-D units to make a Four-Patch unit as shown in Figure 3; press seam in one direction. Repeat to make two Four-Patch units.

Figure 3

5. Sew a Four-Patch unit to an A-B unit to make a row as shown in Figure 4; press seam toward the A-B units. Repeat to make a second row.

Figure 4

6. Join the rows referring to the block drawing to complete one Jacob's Ladder block; press seam in one direction.

7. Repeat steps 3–6 to complete 28 Jacob's Ladder blocks.

Completing the Top

1. Arrange and join seven Jacob's Ladder blocks to make a row as shown in Figure 5; press seams in one direction. Repeat to make four rows.

Make 2   Make 2

Figure 5

2. Join the rows with the E strips referring to the Placement Diagram for positioning; press seams toward E strips.

3. Sew an F strip to the top and bottom of the pieced center; press seams toward F strips.

4. Join the G strips on short ends to make one long strip; press seams open. Subcut strip into two 46½" G strips.

5. Sew the G strips to opposite long sides and H strips to the top and bottom of the pieced center; press seams toward G and H strips to complete the pieced top.

6. Layer, quilt and bind referring to Finishing Your Quilt on page 173. ❖

Polka Dots & Paisleys
Placement Diagram 42" x 54"

Alternating Stars

Bright red and yellow stars march across this pretty quilt.

Design by **CONNIE RAND**

PROJECT SPECIFICATIONS

Skill Level: Intermediate
Quilt Size: 54" x 70"
Block Size: 4" x 4"
Number of Blocks: 80

MATERIALS

- ½ yard red print 1
- ¾ yard yellow print
- ¾ yard red print 2
- 1⅛ yards white print
- 1⅛ yards black solid
- 1⅓ yards black print
- Batting 60" x 76"
- Backing 60" x 76"
- Neutral-color all-purpose thread
- Quilting thread
- Basic sewing tools and supplies

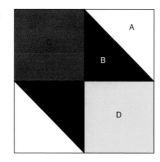

Homeward Bound
4" x 4" Block
Make 80

Cutting

1. Cut six 2⅞" by fabric width strips white print; subcut strips into (80) 2⅞" A squares.

2. Cut (11) 1½" by fabric width F strips white print.

3. Cut six 2⅞" by fabric width strips black solid; subcut strips into (80) 2⅞" B squares.

4. Cut seven 2¼" by fabric width strips black solid for binding.

5. Cut (11) 1½" by fabric width E strips black print.

6. Cut (11) 2½" by fabric width G strips black print.

7. Cut five 2½" by fabric width strips red print 1; subcut strips into (80) 2½" C squares.

8. Cut five 2½" by fabric width strips yellow print; subcut strips into (80) 2½" D squares.

> **Tip** **If you place the A and B strips right sides together and press them before subcutting into squares,** the cut squares will stick together so you can draw the line and stitch on each side of the line without pinning.

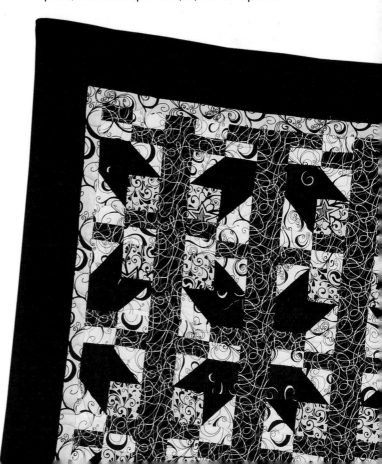

9. Cut six 1½" by fabric width H/I strips yellow print.

10. Cut six 3½" by fabric width J/K strips red print 2.

Completing the Blocks

Note: *Use a ¼" seam allowance throughout.*

1. Draw a diagonal line from corner to corner on the wrong side of each A square.

2. Place an A square right sides together with B; stitch ¼" on each side of the marked line as shown in Figure 1.

3. Cut the stitched unit on the marked line to complete two A-B units, again referring to Figure 1; press seams toward B.

4. Repeat steps 2 and 3 with all A and B squares to complete 160 A-B units.

5. To complete one Homeward Bound block, sew C to the B side of one A-B unit and D to the B side of a second A-B unit as shown in Figure 2; press seams toward C and D.

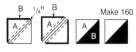

Figure 1

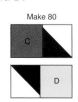

Figure 2

6. Join the A-B-C unit with the A-B-D unit to complete one block, again referring to Figure 2; press seam in one direction.

7. Repeat steps 5 and 6 to complete 80 Homeward Bound blocks.

Completing the Top

1. Sew an E strip to an F strip along length; press seam toward E. Repeat to make 11 E-F strip sets.

2. Subcut strip sets into (176) 2½" E-F segments as shown in Figure 3.

Figure 3

3. Join two E-F segments to make an E-F unit as shown in Figure 4; press seam in one direction. Repeat to make 44 E-F units.

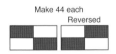

Figure 4

4. Repeat step 3 to make 44 reversed E-F units.

5. Join six E-F units, five reversed E-F units and 10 Homeward Bound blocks to make an X row referring to Figure 5; press seams away from blocks. Repeat to make four X rows.

6. Join six reverse E-F units, five E-F units and 10 Homeward Bound blocks to make a Y row, again referring to Figure 5. Repeat to make four Y rows.

7. Join G strips on short ends to make one long strip; subcut strip into seven 62½" G strips.

8. Join the X and Y rows with G strips to complete the pieced center referring to the Placement Diagram for positioning; press seams toward the G strips.

X Row Make 4   Y Row Make 4

Figure 5

9. Join the H/I strips on short ends to make one long strip; press seams open. Subcut strip into two 62½" H strips and two 48½" I strips.

10. Sew the H strips to opposite long sides and the I strips to the top and bottom of the pieced center; press seams toward the H and I strips.

11. Join the J/K strips on short ends to make one long strip; press seams open. Subcut strip into two 64½" J strips and two 54½" K strips.

12. Sew the J strips to opposite long sides and the K strips to the top and bottom of the pieced center to complete the top; press seams toward the J and K strips.

13. Layer, quilt and bind referring to Finishing Your Quilt on page 173. ✤

Alternating Stars
Placement Diagram 54" x 70"

Oak Lodge

Homespun fabrics give a warm and cozy look to quilts.

Design by ROCHELLE MARTIN

PROJECT SPECIFICATIONS

Skill Level: Beginner
Quilt Size: 57" x 75"
Block Size: 9" x 9"
Number of Blocks: 25

MATERIALS

- ½ yard red plaid
- ¾ yard green homespun
- 1 yard gold plaid
- 1⅞ yards blue plaid
- 2⅛ yards tan plaid
- Batting 63" x 81"
- Backing 63" x 81"
- All-purpose thread to match fabrics
- Quilting thread
- Water-erasable marker

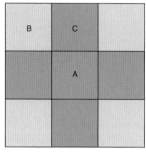

Blue Nine-Patch
9" x 9" Block
Make 4

Red Nine-Patch
9" x 9" Block
Make 9

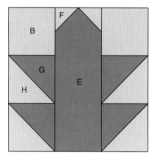

Oak Leaf
9" x 9" Block
Make 12

Cutting

1. Cut two 3½" by fabric width A strips gold plaid.

2. Cut six 2½" by fabric width J/K strips gold plaid.

3. Cut eight 3½" by fabric width B strips tan plaid; subcut two strips into (24) 3½" B squares. Set aside remaining strips for strip sets.

4. Cut three 9½" by fabric width strips tan plaid; subcut strips into (10) 9½" I squares and (24) 2" x 2" F squares.

5. Cut three 3⅞" by fabric width strips tan plaid; subcut strips into (24) 3⅞" squares. Cut each square in half on one diagonal to make 48 H triangles.

6. Cut one 9½" by fabric width strip green homespun; subcut strips into (12) 3½" E strips.

7. Cut three 3⅞" by fabric width strips green homespun; subcut strips into (24) 3⅞" squares. Cut each square in half on one diagonal to make 48 G triangles.

8. Cut three 3½" by fabric width C strips blue plaid.

9. Cut six 4½" by fabric width L/M strips blue plaid.

10. Cut a total of 280" of 2¼"-wide bias strips blue plaid for binding.

11. Cut four 3½" by fabric width D strips red plaid.

Completing the Blue Nine-Patch Blocks

1. Sew a C strip between two B strips along length; press seams toward C.

2. Subcut strip set into eight 3½" B-C units as shown in Figure 1.

Figure 1   **Figure 2**

3. Sew an A strip between two C strips along length; press seams toward C.

4. Subcut strip set into four 3½" A-C units as shown in Figure 2.

5. Sew an A-C unit between two B-C units to complete one Blue Nine-Patch block referring to the block drawing; press seams toward the B-C units.

6. Repeat step 5 to complete four Blue Nine-Patch blocks.

Completing the Red Nine-Patch Blocks

1. Sew a D strip between two B strips along length; press seams toward D strip. Repeat to make two B-D strip sets.

2. Subcut the B-D strip sets into (18) 3½" B-D units as shown in Figure 3.

Figure 3   **Figure 4**

3. Sew an A strip between two D strips along length; press seams toward D strips.

4. Subcut the A-D strip set into nine 3½" A-D units as shown in Figure 4.

5. Sew an A-D unit between two B-D units to complete one Red Nine-Patch block referring to the block drawing; press seams away from the A-D unit.

6. Repeat step 5 to complete nine Red Nine-Patch blocks.

Completing the Oak Leaf Blocks

1. Draw a diagonal line from corner to corner on the wrong side of each F square.

2. Place an F square on one corner of E, matching top and side edges; stitch on the marked line as shown in Figure 5.

Figure 5   **Figure 6**

3. Trim seam allowance to ¼" and press F to the right side, again referring to Figure 5.

4. Repeat steps 2 and 3 on the adjacent corner of E to complete an E-F unit as shown in Figure 6.

5. Repeat steps 2–4 to complete 12 E-F units.

6. Sew G to H along the diagonal to make a G-H unit; press seam toward G. Repeat to make 48 G-H units.

7. To complete one Oak Leaf block, join two G-H units with B to make a side row as shown in Figure 7; press seams toward B. Repeat to make two side rows.

Figure 7

8. Sew a side row to opposite sides of an E-F unit to complete one Oak Leaf block referring to the block drawing; press seams toward the E-F unit.

9. Repeat steps 7 and 8 to complete 12 Oak Leaf blocks.

Completing the Top

1. Join two each Red Nine-Patch and Oak Leaf blocks with an I square to make a W row as shown in Figure 8; press seams toward I and the Nine-Patch blocks. Repeat to make two W rows.

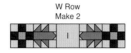

W Row
Make 2

Figure 8

2. Join one Blue Nine-Patch block with two Oak Leaf blocks and two I squares to make an X row as shown in Figure 9; press seams toward I. Repeat to make two X rows.

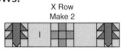

X Row
Make 2

Figure 9

3. Join one Oak Leaf block with two Red Nine-Patch blocks and two I squares to make a Y row as shown in Figure 10; press seams toward I and the Oak Leaf block. Repeat to make two Y rows.

Y Row
Make 2

Figure 10

4. Join one Red Nine-Patch block with two each Blue Nine-Patch and Oak Leaf blocks to make a Z row as shown in Figure 11; press seams toward the Oak Leaf blocks.

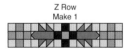

Z Row
Make 1

Figure 11

5. Arrange and join the W, X, Y and Z rows referring to the Placement Diagram to complete the quilt center; press seams in one direction.

6. Join the J/K strips on short ends to make one long strip; press seams open. Subcut strip into two 63½" J strips and two 49½" K strips.

7. Sew a J strip to opposite long sides and K strips to the top and bottom of the pieced center; press seams toward J and K strips.

8. Join the L/M strips on short ends to make one long strip; press seams open. Subcut strip into two 67½" L strips and two 57½" M strips.

9. Sew an L strip to opposite long sides and M strips to the top and bottom of the pieced center to complete the pieced top; press seams toward L and M strips.

10. Layer, quilt and bind referring to Finishing Your Quilt on page 173. ***Note:*** *The acorn quilting design given on page 147 was used in the I squares. Refer to photo of quilt for positioning of design.* ❖

Oak Lodge
Placement Diagram 57" x 75"

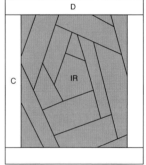

Sophisticated Crazy Patch

You can still have symmetry and order in a crazy quilt.

Design by **NANCY VASILCHIK**

PROJECT SPECIFICATIONS

Skill Level: Beginner
Quilt Size: 48" x 69"
Block Size: 13" x 15"
Number of Blocks: 12

MATERIALS

- 6 fat quarters black-with-white prints
- 6 fat quarters white-with-black prints
- ¾ yard black-and-white print
- ⅞ yard white solid
- 1⅝ yards bleached muslin
- 1⅞ yards black solid
- Batting 54" x 75"
- Backing 54" x 75"
- All-purpose thread to match fabrics
- Black and white decorative threads
- Quilting thread
- 2⅓ yards lightweight tear-off fabric stabilizer
- Water-erasable marker or chalk pencil
- Basic sewing tools and supplies

Cutting

1. Prepare template for I using pattern given (page 147); transfer centering lines to template.

2. Stack the white-with-black fat quarters right side up to make a white set.

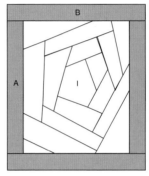

White/Black Crazy
13" x 15" Block
Make 6

Black/White Crazy
13" x 15" Block
Make 6

3. Place the template on the white set and cut as shown in Figure 1; cut the remainder of the stack into strips as marked in Figure 1, starting cutting with the first measurement and increasing or decreasing size to the opposite side as indicated in Figure 1. Transfer the positioning lines to the I pieces using a water-erasable marker or chalk pencil.

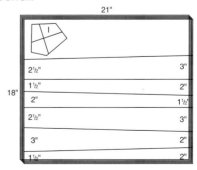

Figure 1

4. Repeat steps 2 and 3 with the black-with-white fat quarters, reversing the I template as shown in Figure 2.

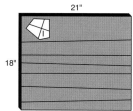

21"

18"

Figure 2

5. Cut two 2" x 60½" E strips along the length of the black solid.

6. Cut two 2" x 42½" F strips along the length of the black solid.

7. Cut one 12½" by remaining fabric width strip black solid; subcut strip into (12) 2" A strips.

8. Cut one 13½" by remaining fabric width strip black solid; subcut strip into (12) 2" B strips.

9. Cut eight 2¼" by remaining fabric width strips black solid for binding.

10. Cut one 12½" by fabric width strip white solid; subcut strip into (12) 2" C strips.

11. Cut one 13½" by fabric width strip white solid; subcut strip into (12) 2" D strips.

12. Cut six 3½" by fabric width G/H strips black-and-white print.

13. Cut four 13" by fabric width strips bleached muslin; subcut strips into (12) 11" muslin base rectangles.

Completing the Blocks

1. Draw a horizontal and vertical line through the center of each muslin base as shown in Figure 3.

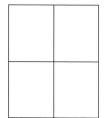

Figure 3

2. To complete one white/black unit, pin one white-with-black I square on a muslin base, matching the lines on the muslin with the lines on I as shown in Figure 4.

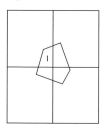

Figure 4

3. Using all white-with-black strips, select one strip; place it right sides together with the pinned I piece extending strip a little at the beginning end as shown in Figure 5.

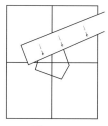

Figure 5   **Figure 6**

4. Stitch using a ¼" seam. Trim the strip to extend a bit beyond the edge of I; press the strip to the right side as shown in Figure 6.

5. Continue adding strips around the sides of I until all sides of I are covered as shown in Figure 7.

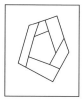

Figure 7

6. Continue adding strips around the center in this manner until the muslin base is covered. *Note: Outer pieces will extend past the muslin.*

7. Turn the completed piece over and trim excess even with the muslin base.

8. Repeat steps 2–7 to complete six white/black units.

9. Repeat steps 2–7 with black-with-white fabrics to complete six black/white units referring to the block drawing.

10. Cut (12) 11" x 13" rectangles lightweight, tear-off fabric stabilizer.

11. Pin a piece of stabilizer to the wrong side of each unit.

12. Using black decorative thread on the white/black units and white decorative thread on the black/white units, add a decorative machine stitch on each seam.

13. After decorative stitching is complete, trim each unit to 10½" x 12½". Remove fabric stabilizer.

14. Sew an A strip to opposite sides and B strips to the top and bottom of each white/black unit to complete the White/Black blocks; press seams toward A and B strips.

15. Sew a C strip to opposite sides and D strips to the top and bottom of each black/white unit to complete the Black/White blocks; press seams toward C and D strips.

Completing the Top

1. Sew a Black/White block between two White/Black blocks to make an X row; press seams toward the White/Black blocks. Repeat to make two X rows.

2. Sew a White/Black block between two Black/White blocks to make a Y row; press seams toward White/Black block. Repeat to make two Y rows.

> **Tip** **Test decorative stitches on a scrap of fabric. This stitching is important because it gives definition to each strip, since all fabrics in each block are of the same value.** Rayon thread gives a nice sheen with stitches that have heavy coverage. For lighter thread coverage, use a 30-weight thread; it will show more dramatically.

3. Join the X and Y rows referring to the Placement Diagram to complete the pieced center; press seams in one direction.

4. Sew an E strip to opposite long sides and F strips to the top and bottom of the pieced center; press seams toward E and F strips.

5. Join the G/H strips on short ends to make one long strip; subcut strip into two 63½" G strips and two 48½" H strips.

6. Sew a G strip to opposite long sides and H strips to the top and bottom of the pieced center; press seams toward G and H strips to complete the pieced top.

7. Layer, quilt and bind referring to Finishing Your Quilt on page 173. ✢

Template on page 147

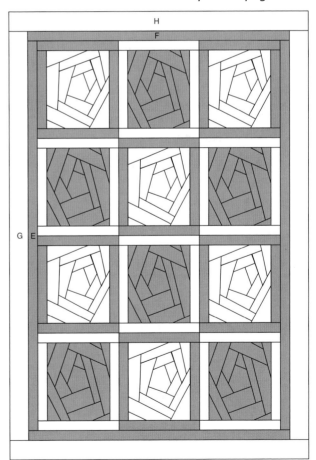

Sophisticated Crazy Patch
Placement Diagram 48" x 69"

Shadow Circles

All straight-edge pieces give the illusion of double circles in this lap-size quilt.

Design by **SUE HARVEY & SANDY BOOBAR**

PROJECT SPECIFICATIONS

Skill Level: Intermediate
Quilt Size: 52" x 70"
Block Size: 18" x 18"
Number of Blocks: 6

MATERIALS

- ⅞ yard light floral
- ⅞ yard cream tonal
- 1 yard dark brown tonal
- 1¼ yards dark floral
- 2 yards blue tonal
- Batting 58" x 76"
- Backing 58" x 76"
- Neutral-color all-purpose thread
- Quilting thread
- Basic sewing tools and supplies

Cutting

1. Cut two 9½" by fabric width strips light floral; subcut strips into six 9½" A squares.

2. Cut two 3½" by fabric width strips light floral. Prepare a template for H using the pattern given. Place the template on the strips and cut 24 H pieces as shown in Figure 1.

3. Cut two 3½" by fabric width strips blue tonal; subcut strips into (24) 3½" B squares.

4. Cut three 3⅞" by fabric width strips blue tonal; subcut strips into (24) 3⅞" squares. Cut each square in half on one diagonal to make 48 C triangles.

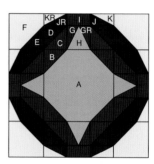

Shadow Circles
18" x 18" Block
Make 6

5. Cut three 3½" by fabric width strips blue tonal. Prepare a template for the G/J/K piece using the pattern given. Place the template on the strips and cut 24 each G and GR pieces, again referring to Figure 1.

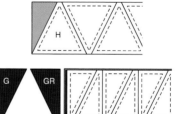

Figure 1

6. Cut two 2" by fabric width strips blue tonal; subcut strips into (24) 3½" I rectangles.

7. Cut two 2½" x 40½" M strips blue tonal.

8. Cut three 2½" by fabric width L strips blue tonal.

9. Cut seven 2¼" by fabric width strips blue tonal for binding.

10. Cut three 3⅞" by fabric width strips dark brown tonal; subcut strips into (24) 3⅞" squares. Cut each square in half on one diagonal to make 48 D triangles.

11. Cut two 3½" by fabric width strips dark brown tonal; subcut strips into (24) 3½" E squares.

12. Cut three 3½" by fabric width strips dark brown tonal. Place the G/J/K template on the strips and cut 24 each J and JR pieces.

13. Cut three 5" by fabric width strips cream tonal; subcut strips into (24) 5" F squares.

14. Cut three 3½" by fabric width strips cream tonal. Place the G/J/K template on the strips and cut 24 each K and KR pieces.

15. Cut six 6½" by fabric width N/O strips dark floral.

Piecing the Units

1. Mark a diagonal line from corner to corner on the wrong side of each B and E square.

2. Place a B square on each corner of an A square as shown in Figure 2; stitch on the marked lines, trim seam allowance to ¼" and press B to the right side to complete one A-B unit. Repeat to make six A-B units.

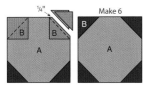

Figure 2   **Figure 3**

3. Repeat step 2 with an E square on one corner of each F square to complete 24 E-F units as shown in Figure 3.

4. Sew C to D on the diagonal to make a C-D unit as shown in Figure 4; press seam toward D. Repeat to complete 48 C-D units.

Figure 4

5. Sew G to one angled edge of H as shown in Figure 5; press seam toward G. Repeat with a GR on the remaining angled edge of H to complete one G-H unit, again referring to Figure 5; press seam toward GR. Repeat to complete 24 G-H units.

Figure 5   **Figure 6**

6. Sew J to K and JR to KR as shown in Figure 6; press seams toward J and JR. Repeat to make 24 each J-K and JR-KR units.

Completing the Shadow Circles Blocks

1. To complete one Shadow Circles Block, sew a G-H unit between two C-D units as shown in Figure 7; press seams toward C-D. Repeat to make four pieced strips.

Figure 7   **Figure 8**

2. Sew I between one each J-K and JR-KR units as shown in Figure 8; press seams toward I. Repeat to make four pieced strips.

3. Join a pieced strip from step 1 with a pieced strip from step 2 to make a side unit as shown in Figure 9; press seams toward the G-H unit strip. Repeat to make four side units.

Figure 9   **Figure 10**

4. Sew a side unit to two opposite sides of an A-B unit to make the block center row as shown in Figure 10; press seams toward the A-B unit.

5. Sew an E-F unit to each end of the remaining side units to make the top and bottom rows, again referring to Figure 10; press seams toward the E-F units.

6. Sew the center row between the top and bottom rows to complete one Shadow Circles block referring to the block drawing for positioning; press seams toward the A-B unit.

7. Repeat steps 1–6 to complete six Shadow Circles blocks.

Completing the Quilt Top

1. Join two Shadow Circles blocks to make a row; press seam open. Repeat to make three rows.

2. Join the rows to complete the pieced center; press seams open.

3. Join the L strips on the short ends to make a long strip; press seams to one side. Cut the strip into two 54½" L strips.

4. Sew the L strips to opposite long sides and M strips to the top and bottom of the pieced center; press seams toward the L and M strips.

5. Repeat step 3 with N/O strips and cut two 58½" N strips and two 52½" O strips.

6. Sew the N strips to opposite long sides and O strips to the top and bottom of the pieced center to complete the top; press seams toward N and O strips.

7. Layer, quilt and bind referring to Finishing Your Quilt on page 173. ✤

Shadow Circles
Placement Diagram 52" x 70"

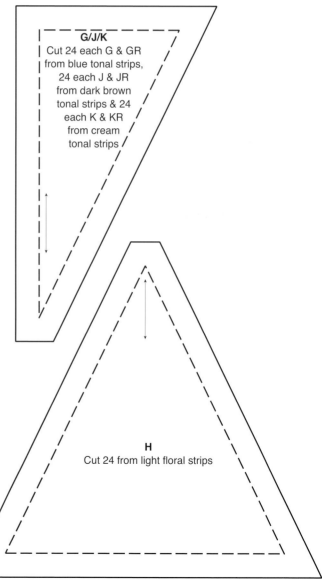

G/J/K
Cut 24 each G & GR from blue tonal strips, 24 each J & JR from dark brown tonal strips & 24 each K & KR from cream tonal strips

H
Cut 24 from light floral strips

Friendship Forest

Buy yardage or use scraps of green, brown and cream or white fabrics to create blocks with variety.

Design by **JULIE WEAVER**

PROJECT SPECIFICATIONS

Skill Level: Beginner
Quilt Size: 48" x 56"
Block Size: 8" x 8"
Number of Blocks: 24

MATERIALS

- ⅛ yard each 24 different green fabrics
- ⅛ yard each 24 different brown fabrics
- ⅛ yard each 24 different cream/white/tan fabrics
- ¾ yard brown print
- 1 yard green print
- Batting 54" x 62"
- Backing 54" x 62"
- All-purpose thread to match fabrics
- Quilting thread
- Basic sewing tools and supplies

Cutting

1. Cut one 2½" by fabric width strip from each green fabric; subcut each strip into four 4½" A rectangles.

2. Cut one 2½" by fabric width strip from each cream/white/tan fabric; subcut each strip into eight 2½" B squares and eight 2" C rectangles.

3. Cut one 1½" by fabric width strip from each brown fabric; subcut each strip into four 2½" D rectangles.

4. Cut four 2" x 40½" E strips and four 2" x 32½" G strips green print.

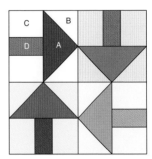

Friendship Forest
8" x 8" Block
Make 24

5. Cut six 2¼" by fabric width strips green print for binding.

6. Cut two 5½" x 40½" F strips and two 5½" x 32½" H strips brown print.

Completing the Blocks

1. Mark a diagonal line from corner to corner on the wrong side of each B square.

2. To complete one Friendship Forest block, select two each same-fabric B squares and C rectangles.

3. Place a B square on one end of A and stitch on the marked line as shown in Figure 1; trim seam to ¼" and press B to the right side, again referring to Figure 1.

Figure 1

4. Repeat with the second matching B square on the remaining end of A to complete one A-B unit as shown in Figure 2.

Figure 2

Figure 3

5. Sew D between two matching C rectangles to make a C-D unit as shown in Figure 3; press seams toward D.

6. Sew the A-B unit to the C-D unit to complete one tree unit as shown in Figure 4; press seam toward the C-D unit.

Figure 4

7. Repeat steps 2–6 to make four tree units.

8. Join two tree units to make a row as shown in Figure 5; press seam in one direction. Repeat to make two rows.

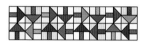

Figure 5

9. Join the two rows referring to the block drawing to complete one Friendship Forest block; press seam in one direction.

10. Repeat steps 2–9 to complete 24 Friendship Forest blocks.

Completing the Top

1. Select four Friendship Forest blocks; join as shown in Figure 6 to make one row. Press seams in one direction. Repeat to make five rows, pressing seams in half the rows in the opposite direction.

Figure 6

2. Join the rows with seams in adjacent rows going in the opposite direction to complete the pieced center; press row seams in one direction.

3. Sew an F strip between two E strips with right sides together along length to make a side strip; press seams toward E strips. Repeat to make two side strips.

4. Sew a side strip to opposite long sides of the pieced center; press seams toward E-F strips.

5. Sew an H strip between two G strips with right sides together along length to make a top strip; press seams toward G. Repeat to make the bottom strip.

6. Sew a Friendship Forest block to each end of each strip; press seams away from blocks.

7. Sew the block strips to the top and bottom of the pieced center to complete the pieced top; press seams toward the block strips.

8. Layer, quilt and bind referring to Finishing Your Quilt on page 173. ✣

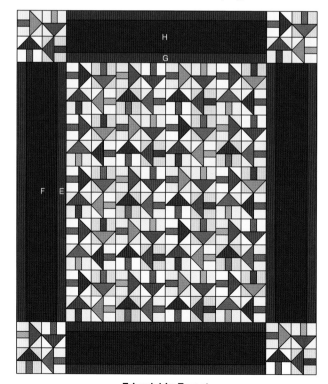

Friendship Forest
Placement Diagram 48" x 56"

Oak Lodge

Continued from page 135

Quilting Motif for I

Place line on fold

Place line on fold

Sophisticated Crazy Patch

Continued from page 139

Top

I
Cut 6 white-with-black prints
Reverse & cut 6
black-with-white prints

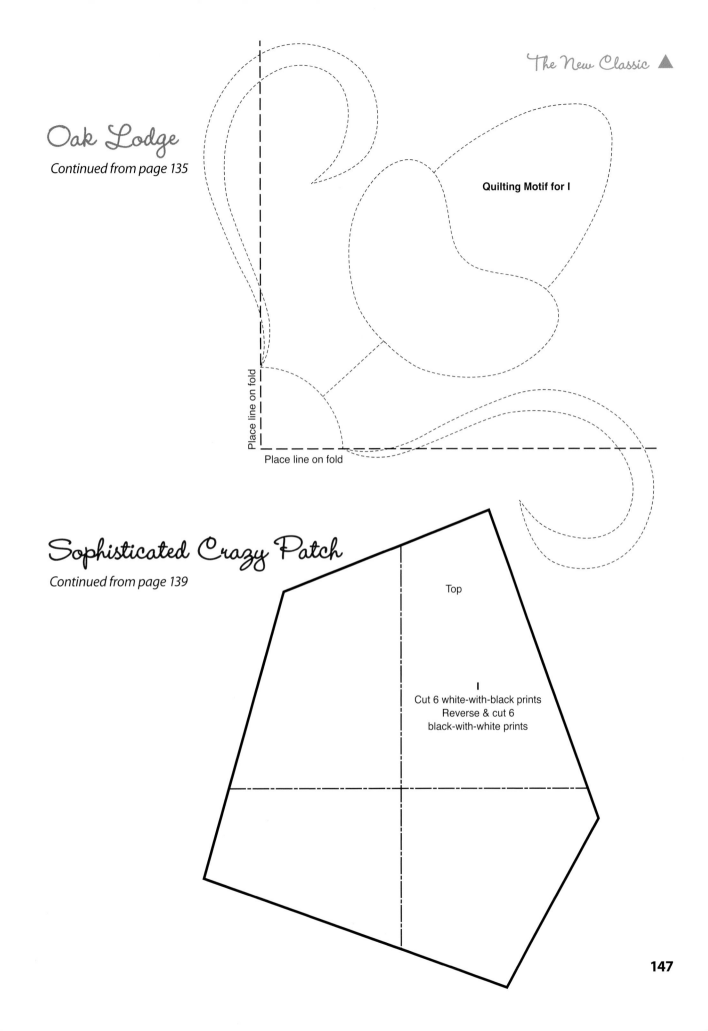

Baby Hugs

Babies and small children need lots of hugs. What better way to hug them than by wrapping them up and cuddling with them in a quilt stitched with love. Baby quilts can be traditional or contemporary, featuring hearts, kites or bright-color blocks. No matter what, they all say, "I love you."

Flying Kites

Kites seem to float in a blue sky on this whimsical little quilt.

Design by **KAREN BLOCHER**

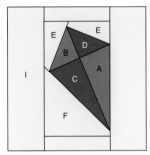

Kite
10" x 10" Block
Make 8

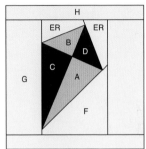

Reverse Kite
10" x 10" Block
Make 8

PROJECT SPECIFICATIONS

Skill Level: Intermediate
Quilt Size: 50" x 50"
Block Size: 10" x 10"
Number of Blocks: 16

MATERIALS

- 8 (10" x 10") bright print squares
- 8 (10" x 10") contrasting tonal/mottled/ near-print squares
- ⅝ yard blue mottled
- 1 yard blue kite print
- 1⅞ yards blue-sky mottled
- Batting 56" x 56"
- Backing 56" x 56"
- All-purpose thread to match fabrics
- Quilting thread
- 16 (12") lengths assorted rickrack to match bright prints
- Pinking shears
- Basic sewing tools and supplies

Cutting

1. Select one square each bright print and contrasting fabric; place right sides together. Repeat with all squares to make eight sets.

2. Cut one 3" x 7" rectangle for A and C, one 3¼" square for B and D and one 2" x 2" square for kite tail from one layered set; repeat with all sets.

3. Cut each A/C rectangle, B/D square and kite-tail square in half on one diagonal to make A, B, C and D pieces and kite tails.

4. Cut three 6½" by fabric width strips blue-sky mottled; subcut strips into (16) 3½" E rectangles and eight 6½" F squares. Cut each F square in half on one diagonal to make 16 F triangles. Cut eight E rectangles diagonally from corner to corner to make 16 E triangles as shown in Figure 1. Repeat with remaining E rectangles, cutting from the opposite corner to corner to make 16 ER triangles, again referring to Figure 1.

Figure 1

5. Cut one 5¼" by fabric width strip blue-sky mottled; subcut strip into (16) 1½" J pieces.

6. Cut two 8½" by fabric width strips blue-sky mottled; subcut strips into (16) 3⅛" G strips.

7. Cut two 10½" by fabric width strips blue-sky mottled; subcut strips into (16) 1½" H strips and (16) 3⅛" I strips.

8. Cut two 5½" x 40½" K strips blue kite print.

9. Cut three 5½" by fabric width L strips along the length of the blue kite print.

10. Cut six 2¼" by fabric width binding strips blue mottled.

Completing the Blocks

1. To complete one Kite block, select one each matching A and B piece and one each matching C and D piece.

2. Sew A to C as shown in Figure 2; press seam toward A.

Figure 2   **Figure 3**

3. Sew B to D, again referring to Figure 2; press seam toward B.

4. Sew the B-D unit to the A-C unit to complete a kite unit referring to Figure 3; press seam toward the B-D unit.

5. Stitch E to the D edge of the kite unit, offsetting the larger end of E by ½" as shown in Figure 4; press seam allowance toward E.

Figure 4   **Figure 5**

6. Stitch E to the B edge of the kite unit, offsetting the larger end ½" from the top of the previously stitched E piece as shown in Figure 5; press seam toward E.

7. Offset and stitch an F piece ½" from the edge of the previously stitched E as shown in Figure 6; press seam toward F.

Figure 6

8. Trim excess pieces to make the kite unit 5¼" x 8½", leaving at least ½" below the bottom tip of the kite.

9. Sew a J strip to the top and bottom, and I strips opposite sides of the kite unit to complete one Kite block; press seams toward I and J.

10. Repeat steps 1–9 to complete eight Kite blocks.

11. Repeat steps 1–8 with ER pieces to complete eight reverse Kite units as shown in Figure 7.

Figure 7

12. Sew a G piece to opposite sides and H strips to the top and bottom of each reverse Kite unit to complete eight Reverse Kite blocks, referring to the block drawing; press seams toward G and H strips.

Completing the Top

1. Arrange and join two each Kite and Reverse Kite blocks to make an X row referring to Figure 8; press seams toward Kite blocks. Repeat to make two X rows.

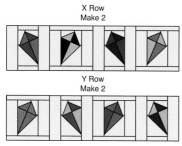

X Row
Make 2

Y Row
Make 2

Figure 8

2. Arrange and join two each Reverse Kite and Kite blocks to make a Y row, again referring to Figure 8; press seams toward Kite blocks. Repeat to make two Y rows.

3. Join the X and Y rows referring to the Placement Diagram to complete the pieced center; press seams toward X rows.

4. Join the L strips on the short ends to make one long strip; press seams open. Subcut strip into two 50½" L strips.

5. Sew a K strip to the top and bottom, and L strips to opposite long sides of the pieced center; press seams toward K and L strips to complete the pieced top.

Completing the Quilt

1. Sandwich the batting between the completed top and prepared backing; pin or baste layers together to hold.

2. Quilt as desired by hand or machine; remove pins or basting. Trim excess backing and batting even with quilt top.

3. Join binding strips on short ends with diagonal seams to make one long strip; trim seams to ¼" and press seams open. Fold the strip in half along length with wrong sides together; press.

4. Sew binding to the right side of the quilt edges, overlapping ends. Fold binding to the back side and stitch in place.

5. Arrange the lengths of rickrack from the bottom point of one kite diagonally into the blue-sky area between kites in the row below or into the bottom border for the bottom rows of blocks as shown in Figure 9 and referring to the Placement Diagram.

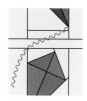

Figure 9   **Figure 10**

6. Referring to Figure 10, arrange the kite-tail triangles point-to-point along the rickrack, matching colors of kite tails with the color of the rickrack, if possible. Stitch through the center of each triangle to complete the quilt, again referring to Figure 10. ❖

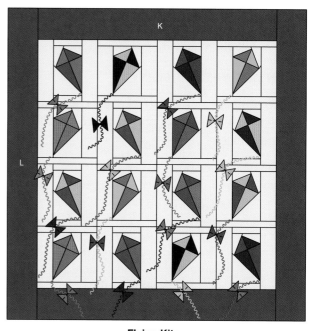

Flying Kites
Placement Diagram 50" x 50"

Pinwheel Daze

It's hard to tell where the blocks end and the sashing begins.

Design by SUE HARVEY & SANDY BOOBAR

PROJECT SPECIFICATIONS

Skill Level: Beginner
Quillow Size: 44" x 60"
Block Size: 12" x 12" and 4" x 12"
Number of Blocks: 6 and 7

MATERIALS

- 7 bright scraps for pinwheels
- ¼ yard multi-colored clown print
- 1 yard white dot
- 1¼ yards green clown print
- 1½ yards blue dot
- Batting 60" x 66"
- Backing 60" x 66"
- Neutral-color all-purpose thread
- Quilting thread
- Basic sewing tools and supplies

Cutting

1. Cut two 2⅞" x 2⅞" squares from each bright scrap; cut each square in half on one diagonal to make four G triangles each scrap.

2. Cut one 4½" by 42" strip multi-colored clown print; subcut strip into eight 4½" A squares.

3. Cut five 6½" by 42" J/K strips green clown print.

4. Cut five 2½" by 42" C strips white dot.

5. Cut three 4½" by 42" strips white dot; subcut strips into (24) 4½" D squares.

6. Cut one 2⅞" by 42" strip white dot; subcut strip into (14) 2⅞" squares. Cut each square in half on one diagonal to make 28 F triangles.

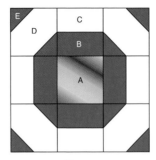

Frame
12" x 12" Block
Make 6

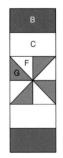

Pinwheel
4" x 12" Block
Make 7

7. Cut five 2½" by 42" B strips blue dot.

8. Cut three 2½" by 42" strips blue dot; subcut strips into (48) 2½" E squares.

9. Cut four 2½" by 42" H/I strips blue dot.

10. Cut six 2¼" by fabric width strips blue dot for binding.

Completing the Frame Blocks

1. Sew a B strip to a C strip with right sides together along the length to make a strip set; press seam toward B. Repeat to make five strip sets.

2. Cut the B-C strip sets into (38) 4½" B-C units as shown in Figure 1; set aside 14 units for Pinwheel blocks.

Figure 1

3. Mark a diagonal line from corner to corner on the wrong side of each E square.

4. Referring to Figure 2, place an E square right sides together on opposite corners of each D square; stitch on the marked lines, trim seam allowances to ¼" and press E to the right side to complete 24 D-E units.

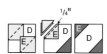

Figure 2

5. Sew a B-C unit to two opposite sides of six A squares to make the block center rows as shown in Figure 3; press seams toward B-C.

Figure 3

6. Sew a D-E unit to each end of 12 B-C units to make the block side rows, again referring to Figure 3; press seams toward B-C.

7. Sew a block center row between two block side rows to complete one Frame block referring to the block drawing for positioning of rows; press seams toward the center row. Repeat to make six blocks.

Completing the Pinwheel Blocks

1. Sew each G triangle to an F triangle along the diagonal; press seams toward G.

2. Select four same-fabric F-G units.

3. Join two F-G units as shown in Figure 4; press seam toward the G side. Repeat.

Figure 4

4. Join the two pieced strips to complete one pinwheel unit; press seam in one direction.

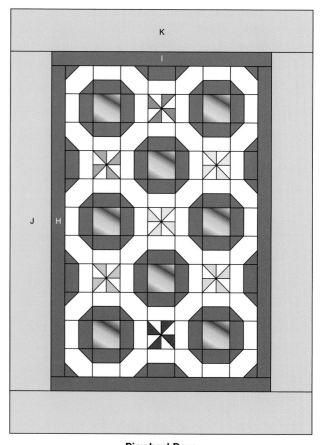

Pinwheel Daze
Placement Diagram 44" x 60"

5. Sew a B-C unit to the top and bottom of the pinwheel unit to complete one block referring to the block drawing for positioning; press seams toward the B-C units.

6. Repeat steps 2–5 to complete seven blocks.

Completing the Top

1. Join two Frame blocks with one Pinwheel block to make an X row as shown in Figure 5; press seams toward the Frame blocks. Repeat to make three X rows.

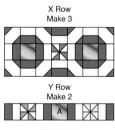

X Row
Make 3

Y Row
Make 2

Figure 5

Continued on page 172

Star of My Heart

Pastel pieced-heart blocks set on point make a perfect baby quilt.

Design by **JULIE WEAVER**

PROJECT SPECIFICATIONS

Skill Level: Advanced
Quilt Size: 48" x 61"
Block Sizes: 8" x 8"
Number of Blocks: 18

MATERIALS

- ¼ yard yellow star print
- ½ yard lavender dot
- ⅝ yard blue dot
- ⅝ yard yellow dot
- ¾ yard pink dot
- 1½ yards green star print
- 1¾ yards white print
- Batting 54" x 67"
- Backing 54" x 67"
- All-purpose thread to match fabrics
- Quilting thread
- Basic sewing tools and supplies

Cutting

1. Cut two 1⅞" by fabric width strips yellow dot; subcut strips into (24) 1⅞" A squares.

2. Cut two 1½" by fabric width strips yellow dot; subcut strips into (48) 1½" C squares.

3. Cut one 1½" by fabric width strip yellow dot; subcut strips into (17) 1½" T squares.

4. Cut one 2⅝" by fabric width strip yellow dot; subcut strip into four 2⅝" squares. Cut each square on both diagonals to make 16 U triangles; discard two.

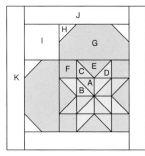

Pink Heart
8" x 8" Block
Make 12

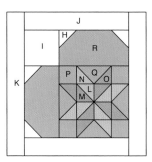

Blue Heart
8" x 8" Block
Make 6

5. Cut two 3½" by fabric width BB strips yellow dot.

6. Cut two 1⅞" by fabric width strips green star print; subcut strips into (24) 1⅞" B squares.

7. Cut two 1½" by fabric width strips green star print; subcut strips into (48) 1½" D squares.

8. Cut two 8½" by fabric width strips green star print; subcut strips into (48) 1½" S strips.

9. Cut three 1½" by fabric width X strips green star print.

10. Cut two 1½" x 40½" Y strips green star print.

11. Cut six 2¼" by fabric width strips green star print for binding.

12. Cut two 2½" by fabric width strips blue dot; subcut strips into (12) 4½" R pieces.

13. Cut three 1½" by fabric width strips blue dot; subcut strips into (24) 2½" Q pieces and (24) 1½" P squares.

14. Cut two 3½" by fabric width CC strips blue dot.

15. Cut one 1⅞" by fabric width strip yellow star print; subcut strips into (12) 1⅞" L squares.

16. Cut one 1½" by fabric width strip yellow star print; subcut strip into (24) 1½" N squares.

17. Cut one 1⅞" by fabric with strip lavender dot; subcut strip into (12) 1⅞" M squares.

18. Cut one 1½" by fabric width strip lavender dot; subcut strip into (24) 1½" O squares.

19. Cut two 3½" by fabric width strips each lavender dot (AA) and pink dot (Z).

20. Cut three 2½" by fabric width strips pink dot; subcut strips into (24) 4½" G pieces.

21. Cut five 1½" by fabric width strips pink dot; subcut strips into (48) 2½" E pieces and (48) 1½" F squares.

22. Cut two 6½" by fabric width strips white print; subcut strips into (36) 1½" J strips.

23. Cut two 8½" by fabric width strips white print; subcut strips into (36) 1½" K strips.

24. Cut two 2½" by fabric width strips white print; subcut strips into (18) 2½" I squares.

25. Cut three 1½" by fabric width strips white print; subcut strips into (72) 1½" H squares.

26. Cut one 12⅝" by fabric width strip white print; subcut strip into three 12⅝" squares. Cut each square on both diagonals to make 12 V triangles; discard 2.

27. Cut one 6½" by fabric width strip white print; subcut strip into two 6½" squares. Cut each square in half on one diagonal to make four W triangles.

Completing the Pink Heart Blocks

1. Draw a diagonal line from corner to corner on the wrong side of each A, C, D and H square.

2. Place an A and B square right sides together; stitch ¼" on each side of the marked line as shown in Figure 1.

Figure 1   **Figure 2**

3. Cut apart on the marked line to make two A-B units as shown in Figure 2; press seam toward A.

4. Repeat steps 2 and 3 to complete 48 A-B units.

5. Place a D square on one end of E and stitch on the marked line as shown in Figure 3; trim seam to ¼" and press D to the right side, again referring to Figure 3.

Figure 3   **Figure 4**

6. Repeat step 5 with C on the opposite end of E to complete a C-D-E unit as shown in Figure 4; press seam toward E.

7. Repeat steps 5 and 6 to complete 48 C-D-E units.

8. To complete one Pink Heart block, join two A-B units to make a row as shown in Figure 5; press seam in one direction. Repeat to make two rows.

Figure 5   **Figure 6**   **Figure 7**

9. Join the two A-B rows to complete the block center as shown in Figure 6; press seam in one direction.

10. Sew a C-D-E unit to opposite sides of the block center to complete the center row as shown in Figure 7; press seams toward the C-D-E unit.

11. Sew an F square to each end of a C-D-E unit to make the top row as shown in Figure 8; press seams toward F squares. Repeat to complete the bottom row.

12. Sew the top and bottom rows to the block center referring to the block drawing to complete the star-design center; press seams away from the center row.

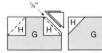

Figure 8   **Figure 9**

13. Place an H square right sides together on two corners of G and stitch on the marked line as shown in Figure 9; trim seams to ¼" and press H to the right side to complete a G-H unit. Repeat to make two G-H units.

14. Sew a G-H unit to one side of the star-design center; press seam toward G-H.

15. Sew I to one end of the remaining G-H unit as shown in Figure 9; press seam toward the H-R unit.

16. Sew the G-H-I unit to the star-design center to make a pieced heart design referring to Figure 10; press seam away from the star-design center.

Figure 10

17. Sew a J strip to the top and bottom, and K strips to opposite sides of the pieced block referring to the block drawing for positioning.

18. Repeat steps 8–17 to complete 12 Pink Heart blocks.

Completing the Blue Heart Blocks

1. Mark a diagonal line from corner to corner on the wrong side of each L, N and O square.

2. To complete six Blue Heart blocks, refer to Figures 1–8 substituting L for A, M for B, Q for E, O for D and N for C to make units referring to Figure 11.

Figure 11   **Figure 12**   **Figure 13**

3. Join the units with P to make rows referring to Figure 12 and steps 8–12 of Completing the Pink Heart Blocks; join the rows to complete the star center.

4. Complete two H-R units as shown in Figure 13.

5. Complete six Blue Heart blocks referring to steps 14–17 of Completing the Pink Heart blocks, substituting the H-R units for the G-H units.

Completing the Top

1. Join two Blue Heart and three Pink Heart blocks with six S strips to make a five-block row as shown in Figure 14; press seams toward S strips. Repeat to make two five-block rows.

2. Join one Blue Heart block with two Pink Heart blocks and four S strips to make a three-block row, again referring to Figure 14; press seams toward S strips. Repeat to make two three-block rows.

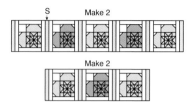

Make 2

Make 2

Figure 14

3. Sew an S strip to opposite sides of each of the remaining Pink Heart blocks as shown in Figure 15; press seams toward S strips. Add V to the S sides, again referring to Figure 15; press seams toward V.

Figure 15   **Figure 16**

4. Sew U to each end of an S strip; press seams toward S. Add W to complete a corner unit as shown in Figure 16; repeat to make two corner units.

5. Join three S strips, two T squares and two U triangles to make a three-unit sashing strip referring to Figure 17; press seams toward S strips. Repeat to make two three-unit sashing strips.

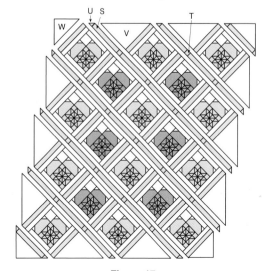

Figure 17

6. Repeat step 5 with five S strips, four T squares and two U triangles to make two five-unit sashing strips, again referring to Figure 17.

7. Repeat step 5 with six S strips, five T squares and two U triangles to make a six-unit sashing strip, again referring to Figure 17.

8. Join the block rows with the sashing strips, corner units and the V and W triangles to complete the pieced center referring to Figure 17.

9. Join the X strips on short ends to make one long strip; press seams open. Subcut strip into two 51½" X strips.

10. Sew an X strip to opposite long sides and Y strips to the top and bottom of the pieced center; press seams toward X and Y strips.

11. Sew a Z strip to an AA strip on the long sides; press seam toward AA strip. Repeat to make two Z-AA strip sets. Subcut strip sets into (17) 4½" Z-AA units as shown in Figure 18.

Figure 18

12. Repeat step 11 with BB and CC strips to make (17) 4½" BB-CC units, again referring to Figure 18.

13. Join five Z-AA units with four BB-CC units as shown in Figure 19; press seams in one direction.

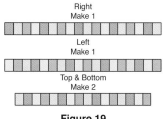

Figure 19

14. Center and sew a row to the right side edge of the pieced center; press seam toward X strips. Trim excess at each end even with the edge of Y.

15. Repeat steps 13 and 14 with five BB-CC units and four Z-AA units, again referring to Figure 19; sew to the left side edge of the pieced center.

16. Join four each Z-AA and BB-CC units to make a strip, again referring to Figure 19; press seams in one direction. Repeat to make two rows.

17. Center and sew a row to the top and bottom of the pieced center; press seams toward Y. Trim excess at each end even with the edge of pieced side strips if neccessary to complete the pieced top.

18. Layer, quilt and bind referring to Finishing Your Quilt on page 173. ❖

Star of My Heart
Placement Diagram 48" x 61"

Playing Jacks

A favorite childhood memory for many people is of times spent playing jacks with friends and family.

Design by **JULIE WEAVER**

PROJECT SPECIFICATIONS

Skill Level: Intermediate
Quilt Size: 40" x 52"
Block Sizes: 4" x 4" and 8" x 8"
Number of Blocks: 34 and 10

MATERIALS

Note: *Fabric is 43" usable width.*
- ⅜ yard green print
- ⅝ yard light blue print
- ⅞ yard dark blue print
- 1 yard cream print
- 1½ yards red print
- Batting 46" x 58"
- Backing 46" x 58"
- All-purpose thread to match fabrics
- Quilting thread
- Basic sewing tools and supplies

Cutting

1. Cut four 1⅞" by fabric width strips light blue print; subcut strips into (68) 1⅞" A squares.

2. Cut five 1½" by fabric width strips light blue print; subcut strips into (136) 1½" D squares.

3. Cut (13) 1½" by fabric width strips cream print; subcut strips into (136) 1½" F squares and (136) 2½" C rectangles.

4. Cut three 3" by fabric width strips cream print; subcut strips into (40) 3" J squares.

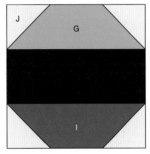

Ball
8" x 8" Block
Make 10

Jacks
4" x 4" Block
Make 34

5. Cut four 1⅞" by fabric width strips red print; subcut strips into (68) 1⅞" B squares.

6. Cut five 1½" by fabric width strips red print; subcut strip into (136) 1½" E squares.

7. Cut one 8½" by fabric width strip red print; subcut strip into (10) 3½" H pieces.

8. Cut two 1½" x 40½" K strips and two 1½" x 30½" L strips red print.

9. Cut two 1½" x 40½" P strips red print.

10. Cut three 1½" by fabric width O strips red print.

11. Cut five 2¼" by fabric width strips red print for binding.

12. Cut one 8½" by fabric width strip green print; subcut strip into (10) 3" G pieces.

13. Cut one 8½" by fabric width strip dark blue print; subcut strip into (10) 3" I pieces.

14. Cut two 4½" x 42½" M strips and two 4½" x 30½" N strips dark blue print.

Completing the Jacks Blocks

1. Draw a diagonal line from corner to corner on the wrong side of each A, D and E square.

2. Place an A and B square right sides together; stitch ¼" on each side of the marked line as shown in Figure 1.

Figure 1   **Figure 2**

3. Cut apart on the marked line to make two A-B units as shown in Figure 2; press seam toward B.

4. Repeat steps 2 and 3 to complete 136 A-B units.

5. Place a D square on one end of C and stitch on the marked line as shown in Figure 3; trim seam to ¼" and press D to the right side, again referring to Figure 3.

Figure 3

6. Repeat step 5 with E on the opposite end of C to complete a C-D-E unit as shown in Figure 4; press seam to E.

Figure 4

7. Repeat steps 5 and 6 to complete 136 C-D-E units.

8. To complete one Jacks block, join two A-B units to make a row as shown in Figure 5; press seam in one direction. Repeat to make two rows.

Figure 5

9. Join the two A-B rows to complete the block center as shown in Figure 6; press seam open to reduce bulk in the center.

Figure 6   **Figure 7**

10. Sew a C-D-E unit to opposite sides of the block center to complete the center row as shown in Figure 7; press seam toward the A-B unit.

11. Sew an F square to each end of a C-D-E unit to make the top row as shown in Figure 8; press seams toward F squares. Repeat to complete the bottom row.

Figure 8

12. Sew the top and bottom rows to the block center referring to the block drawing to complete one Jacks block; press seams away from the center row.

13. Repeat steps 8–12 to complete 34 Jacks blocks.

Completing the Ball Blocks

1. Mark a diagonal line from corner to corner on the wrong side of each J square.

2. To complete one Ball block, sew an H piece between one each G and I pieces as shown in Figure 9; press seams away from H.

Figure 9

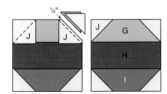

Figure 10

3. Place a J square right sides together on each corner of the G-H-I unit and stitch on the marked line as shown in Figure 10; trim seam to ¼" and press J to the right side to complete one Ball block.

4. Repeat steps 2 and 3 to complete 10 Ball blocks.

Completing the Top

1. Join five Ball blocks to make a Ball row as shown in Figure 11; press seams in one direction. Repeat to make two Ball rows.

Figure 11

2. Join 10 Jacks blocks to make a Jacks row referring to the Placement Diagram; press seams in one direction. Repeat to make three Jacks rows.

3. Join the Ball rows with the Jacks rows to complete the pieced center referring to the Placement Diagram for positioning of rows.

4. Sew a K strip to opposite long sides and L strips to the top and bottom of the pieced center; press seam toward K and L strips.

5. Sew an M strip to opposite long sides of the pieced center; press seams toward M strips.

6. Sew a Jacks block to each end of each N strip; press seams toward N strips. Repeat to make two N/Jacks strips.

7. Sew an N/Jacks strip to the top and bottom of the pieced center; press seams toward N/Jacks strips.

8. Join the O strips on short ends to make one long strip; press seams open. Subcut strip into two 50½" O strips.

9. Sew an O strip to opposite long sides and P strips to the top and bottom of the pieced center; press seams toward O and P strips to complete the pieced top.

10. Layer, quilt and bind referring to Finishing Your Quilt on page 173. ❖

Playing Jacks
Placement Diagram 40" x 52"

Teddy Bears & Hearts

Babies are comforted by the warmth and softness of a quilt.

Design by HOLLY MABUTAS

PROJECT NOTE

If this quilt will be used as a wall hanging, you may add hot-fix crystals to create a little shine on each heart shape and the teddy bear eyes.

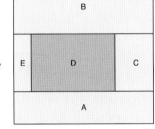

Background
10" x 10" Block
Make 9

PROJECT SPECIFICATIONS

Skill Level: Intermediate
Quilt Size: 30" x 30"
Block Size: 10" x 10"
Number of Blocks: 9

MATERIALS

- 10 different 12" x 12" squares light pastel prints
- 5 different 8" x 10" rectangles brown prints and plaids for bears
- 1 fat quarter pink dot
- ½ yard tan stripe
- Batting 36" x 36"
- Backing 36" x 36"
- All-purpose thread to match fabrics
- Quilting thread
- Black, brown, tan and pink embroidery floss
- Optional: 10 black and 4 pink hot-fix crystals
- Water-erasable marker
- Basic sewing tools and supplies

Cutting

1. Stack two coordinating 12" x 12" light pastel squares; cut the stack into one each 3" x 12" A and 4½" x 12" B rectangles. From the remaining 4½" x 12" stack, cut a 2" x 4½" C, a 6½" x 4½" D and a 3½" x 4½" E as shown in Figure 1. Repeat with remaining fabrics to cut five sets of 10 of each size piece.

Figure 1

2. Cut 2¼"-wide bias strips tan stripe to total 150" for binding.

3. Prepare templates for appliqué shapes using patterns given; cut as directed on each shape, adding a ¼" seam allowance around each piece for hand appliqué.

Completing the Background Blocks

1. Take a D piece from one stacked set and exchange with a D piece in the same stack. **Note:** *The A, B, C and E pieces in one block will be the same fabric and the D piece will be the fabric from the second stack.*

2. Sew C and E to opposite sides of D to make a C-D-E row as shown in Figure 2; press seams toward D.

Figure 2

Figure 3

3. Align one end of A and B with the C end of the C-D-E row and stitch to complete a block unit as shown in Figure 3; press seams away from A and B.

4. Repeat steps 2 and 3 with the remaining pieces in the first stacked set.

5. Repeat steps 1–3 with all stacked sets to complete nine block units. Set aside remaining set of pieces for another use or stitch another block unit, which may be used to make a label for the back of the quilt.

6. Trim each block unit to 10½" x 10½" to complete nine Background blocks.

Completing the Appliqué & Embroidery

1. Transfer embroidery patterns to the heart and bear body shapes using patterns given and a water-erasable marker.

2. Using 3 strands of pink embroidery floss and a stem stitch, stitch the words on the heart shapes.

Note: *If using a crystal on each heart, add at this time referring to manufacturer's instructions.*

3. Using 3 strands of brown or tan embroidery floss and a long running stitch, add details to bear bodies.

4. Using 3 strands black embroidery floss and a French knot, add eyes to each bear. **Note:** *If using crystals for eyes, add at this time referring to manufacturer's instructions.*

5. Turn under the seam allowance on all appliqué pieces using your favorite method.

6. Arrange a heart shape on four of the Background blocks referring to the Placement Diagram for positioning; when satisfied with placement, hand- or machine-stitch in place.

7. Repeat step 6 with bear motifs, layering in numerical order as marked on patterns and referring to the Placement Diagram for positioning. **Note:** *Notice the positioning of the head, legs and arms on the bear motifs is different from block to block, making them look like they are in motion.*

Teddy Bears & Hearts
Placement Diagram 30" x 30"

Completing the Top

1. Arrange and join the teddy bear and heart-motif Background blocks in three rows of three blocks each referring to the Placement Diagram for positioning; press seams in adjacent rows in opposite directions.

2. Join the rows to complete the pieced top; press seams in one direction.

3. Layer, quilt and bind referring to Finishing Your Quilt on page 173. ❖

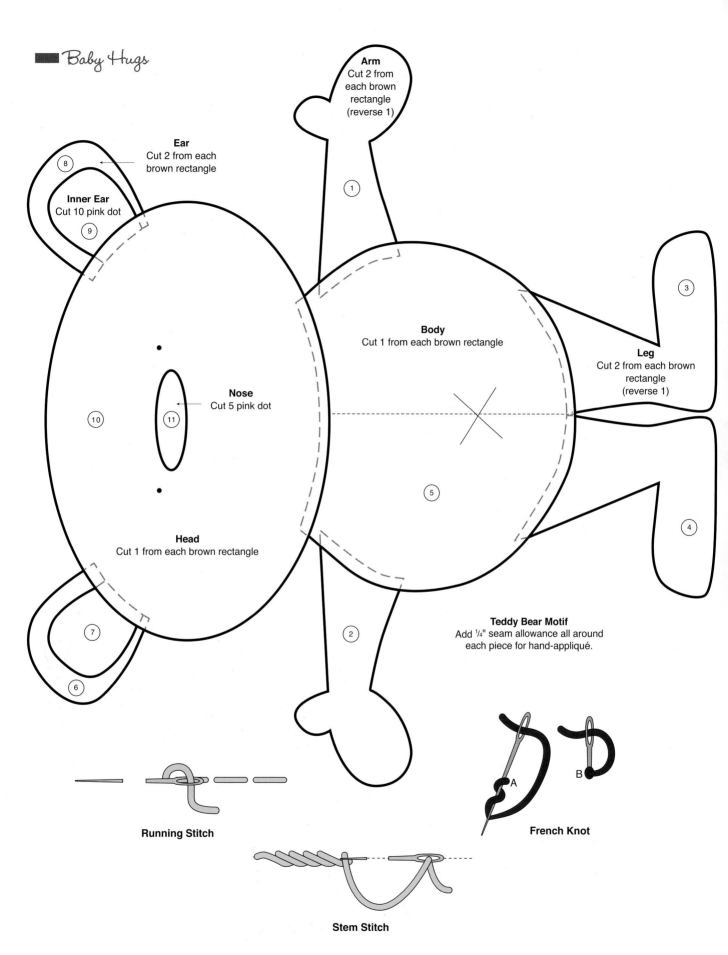

Arm
Cut 2 from
each brown
rectangle
(reverse 1)

①

Ear
Cut 2 from each
brown rectangle

⑧

Inner Ear
Cut 10 pink dot

⑨

③

Body
Cut 1 from each brown rectangle

Leg
Cut 2 from each brown
rectangle
(reverse 1)

Nose
Cut 5 pink dot

⑩   ⑪

⑤

④

Head
Cut 1 from each brown rectangle

⑦

Teddy Bear Motif
Add ¼" seam allowance all around
each piece for hand-appliqué.

②

⑥

Running Stitch

A

B

French Knot

Stem Stitch

Heart
Cut 4 pink dot

hugs

giggle

happy

oh bear

Words

Oh Baby!

A pretty pink print with purple will brighten up any little one's room.

Design by **CONNIE KAUFFMAN**

PROJECT SPECIFICATIONS

Skill Level: Beginner
Quilt Size: 32" x 36"

MATERIALS

- ½ yard purple tonal
- ½ yard white print
- ⅞ yard pink print
- Batting 38" x 42"
- Backing 38" x 42"
- Neutral-color all-purpose thread
- Quilting thread
- Basic sewing tools and supplies

Cutting

1. Cut one 15½" by fabric width strip pink print; subcut strip into one 11½" A rectangle. Trim the remainder of the strip into two 7" by remaining fabric width strips; subcut each strip into one 7" x 22" G strip and one 7" F square.

2. Cut one 7" by fabric width strip pink print; subcut strip into two two 19½" H strips.

3. Cut one 4½" by fabric width strip pink print; subcut strip into two 4½" D squares.

4. Cut two 4½" by fabric width strips white print; subcut strips into four 15½" E strips.

5. Cut one 4½" by fabric width strip white print; subcut strip into four 7" B rectangles.

6. Cut one 2½" by fabric width strip purple tonal; subcut strip into (16) 2½" C squares.

7. Cut four 2¼" by fabric width strips purple tonal for binding.

Completing the Top

1. Mark a diagonal line from corner to corner on the wrong side of each C square.

2. Place one C square right sides together on one corner of a B rectangle and stitch on the marked line as shown in Figure 1; trim seam to ¼" and press C to the right side, again referring to Figure 1.

Figure 1   **Figure 2**

3. Repeat step 2 with another C on the same end of B to complete one B-C unit as shown in Figure 2.

4. Repeat steps 2 and 3 to complete four B-C units.

5. Repeat steps 2 and 3 with C and E to complete four C-E units referring to Figure 3.

Figure 3

6. Sew a C-E unit to opposite long sides of A as shown in Figure 4; press seams toward A.

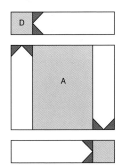

Figure 4

7. Add D to the C end of the two remaining C-E units; press seams toward D. Sew the D-C-E units to the top and bottom of the stitched unit, again referring to Figure 4; press seams toward A.

8. Sew a B-C unit to one end of H as shown in Figure 5; press seam toward H. Repeat to make two H-B-C units.

9. Sew an H-B-C unit to opposite sides of pieced center unit referring to the Placement Diagram for positioning; press seams toward the H-B-C unit.

10. Join F and G with a B-C unit, again referring to Figure 5; press seams toward F and G. Repeat to make two F-B-C-G strips. Sew a strip to the top and bottom of the pieced center to complete the pieced top; press seams toward the F-B-C-G strips.

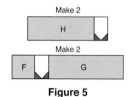

Figure 5

11. Layer, quilt and bind referring to Finishing Your Quilt on page 173. ✤

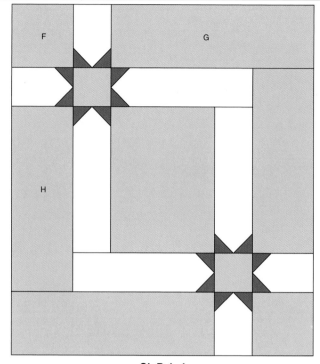

Oh Baby!
Placement Diagram 32" x 36"

Pinwheel Daze

Continued from page 155

2. Join two Pinwheel blocks with an A square to make a Y row, again referring to Figure 5; press seams toward A. Repeat to make two Y rows.

3. Join the rows to complete the pieced center referring to the Placement Diagram for positioning of rows; press seams toward the X rows.

4. Join the H/I strips on the short ends to make one long strip; press seams open. Subcut strip into two 44½" H strips and two 32½" I strips.

5. Sew the H strips to opposite long sides and I strips to the top and bottom of the pieced center; press seams toward H and I strips.

6. Join the J/K strips on short ends to make one long strip; press seams open. Subcut strip into two 48½" J strips and two 44½" K strips.

7. Sew the J to opposite long sides and K strips to the top and bottom of the pieced center to complete the top; press seams toward J and K strips.

8. Layer, quilt and bind referring to Finishing Your Quilt on page 173. ✤

Finishing Your Quilt

Step 1. Sandwich the batting between the completed top and prepared backing; pin or baste layers together to hold. **_Note:_** _If using basting spray to hold layers together, refer to instructions on the product container for use._

Step 2. Quilt as desired by hand or machine, remove pins or basting. Trim excess backing and batting even with quilt top.

Step 3. Join binding strips on short ends to make one long strip. Fold the strip in half along length with wrong sides together, press.

Step 4. Sew binding to quilt edges, mitering corners and overlapping ends. Fold binding to the back side and stitch in place to finish. ❖

Metric Conversion Charts

Metric Conversions

yards	x	.9144	=	metres (m)
yards	x	91.44	=	centimetres (cm)
inches	x	2.54	=	centimetres (cm)
inches	x	25.40	=	millimetres (mm)
inches	x	.0254	=	metres (m)

centimetres	x	.3937	=	inches
metres	x	1.0936	=	yards

Standard Equivalents

⅛ inch	=	3.20 mm	=	0.32 cm
¼ inch	=	6.35 mm	=	0.635 cm
⅜ inch	=	9.50 mm	=	0.95 cm
½ inch	=	12.70 mm	=	1.27 cm
⅝ inch	=	15.90 mm	=	1.59 cm
¾ inch	=	19.10 mm	=	1.91 cm
⅞ inch	=	22.20 mm	=	2.22 cm
1 inch	=	25.40 mm	=	2.54 cm
⅛ yard	=	11.43 cm	=	0.11 m
¼ yard	=	22.86 cm	=	0.23 m
⅜ yard	=	34.29 cm	=	0.34 m
½ yard	=	45.72 cm	=	0.46 m
⅝ yard	=	57.15 cm	=	0.57 m
¾ yard	=	68.58 cm	=	0.69 m
⅞ yard	=	80.00 cm	=	0.80 m
1 yard	=	91.44 cm	=	0.91 m

1⅛ yards	=	102.87 cm	=	1.03 m
1¼ yards	=	114.30 cm	=	1.14 m
1⅜ yards	=	125.73 cm	=	1.26 m
1½ yards	=	137.16 cm	=	1.37 m
1⅝ yards	=	148.59 cm	=	1.49 m
1¾ yards	=	160.02 cm	=	1.60 m
1⅞ yards	=	171.44 cm	=	1.71 m
2 yards	=	182.88 cm	=	1.83 m
2⅛ yards	=	194.31 cm	=	1.94 m
2¼ yards	=	205.74 cm	=	2.06 m
2⅜ yards	=	217.17 cm	=	2.17 m
2½ yards	=	228.60 cm	=	2.29 m
2⅝ yards	=	240.03 cm	=	2.40 m
2¾ yards	=	251.46 cm	=	2.51 m
2⅞ yards	=	262.88 cm	=	2.63 m
3 yards	=	274.32 cm	=	2.74 m
3⅛ yards	=	285.75 cm	=	2.86 m
3¼ yards	=	297.18 cm	=	2.97 m
3⅜ yards	=	308.61 cm	=	3.09 m
3½ yards	=	320.04 cm	=	3.20 m
3⅝ yards	=	331.47 cm	=	3.31 m
3¾ yards	=	342.90 cm	=	3.43 m
3⅞ yards	=	354.32 cm	=	3.54 m
4 yards	=	365.76 cm	=	3.66 m
4⅛ yards	=	377.19 cm	=	3.77 m
4¼ yards	=	388.62 cm	=	3.89 m
4⅜ yards	=	400.05 cm	=	4.00 m
4½ yards	=	411.48 cm	=	4.11 m
4⅝ yards	=	422.91 cm	=	4.23 m
4¾ yards	=	434.34 cm	=	4.34 m
4⅞ yards	=	445.76 cm	=	4.46 m
5 yards	=	457.20 cm	=	4.57 m

Photo Index

Photo Index

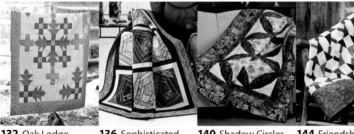

Special Thanks

Please join us in thanking the talented designers listed below.

Ann Anderson
Interlocking Blocks, 72

Karen Blocher
Flirty Thirties, 46
Flying Kites, 149

**Brenda Connelly &
Barbara Miller**
Cabin in the Orchard, 64
Diamonds in the Garden, 107

Phyllis Dobbs
Gypsy Wind, 76

Julia Dunn
Woodland Acres, 57

Connie Ewbank
Long Logs, 60

**Lucy A. Fazely &
Michael L. Burns**
Hexagon Beauty, 10

Susan Fletcher
Summer Trellis, 22

**Sue Harvey & Sandy
Boobar**
Floating Frames, 94
Shadow Circles, 140
Pinwheel Daze, 153

Julie Higgins
Plum Jelly Stars, 39
Luscious Jiffy Cake Quilt &
    Pillow Shams, 68

Connie Kauffman
Dust Storm Bed Warmer, 13
Scrappy Confusion, 30
Spring, 51
Starry Stripes, 89
Interwoven Melodies, 123
Oh Baby!, 170

Konda Luckau
Purple Pandemonium, 43

Holly Mabutas
Teddy Bears & Hearts, 165

Chris Malone
Honey Bees Buzz, 98
Crazy Patch Roses, 101
Patchwork Flowers, 114
Summer Charm, 119

Rochelle Martin
Oak Lodge, 132

Connie Rand
Alternating Stars, 129

Jill Reber
Foot-of-the-Bed Warmer, 27
Polka Dots & Paisleys, 126

Judith Sandstrom
Well-Connected Stars, 84

Lynn Schiefelbein
Hopscotch, 36

Christine Schultz
Salad, 80

Nancy Vasilchik
Sophisticated Crazy
    Patch, 136

Julie Weaver
Bed of Roses, 6
Diamond Flush, 18
Color Splash, 54
Friendship Forest, 144
Star of My Heart, 156
Playing Jacks, 161

Credits

Page 6: Bed of Roses—
Thermore batting from Hobbs.

Page 10: Hexagon Beauty—
Spice Market fabric collection
from Exclusively Quilters, Warm
& White cotton batting from
The Warm Company, Dual
Duty XP and Star Multicolored
Quilting thread from Coats,
and Quilt Basting Spray from
Sullivans USA.

**Page 13: Dust Storm Bed
Warmer—**Blendable and
Cotton thread from Sulky of
America, and Poly Cotton
Fusible batting from Hobbs.

Page 18: Diamond Flush—
Thermore batting from Hobbs.

**Page 27: Foot-of-the-Bed
Warmer—**Moda fabrics, Warm
& Natural cotton batting from
The Warm Company, and
Master Piece 45 ruler and
Static Stickers.

Page 30: Scrappy Confusion—
Warm & Natural cotton batting
from The Warm Company.

Page 39: Plum Jelly Stars—
Gypsy Rose fabric collection
from Moda.

Page 51: Spring—Fabric
from Deb Strain's Fresh fabric
collection by Deb Strain for
Moda, Blendable cotton thread
from Sulky of America, and
Warm & Natural cotton batting
from The Warm Company

Page 54: Color Splash—
Thermore batting from Hobbs.

**Page 68: Luscious Jiffy Cake
Quilt & Pillow Shams—**
Harmony Collection by Jan
Patek for Moda.

Page 76: Gypsy Wind—Gypsy
Breeze fabric collection by
Marie Osmond for Quilting
Treasures, Warm & Natural
cotton batting from The Warm
Company, and Blendables
cotton thread from Sulky of
America.

**Page 84: Well-Connected
Stars—**Califon fabric collection
by Mark Lipinski for Northcott.

Page 89: Starry Stripes—Warm
& Natural cotton batting and
Lite Steam-A-Seam fusible web
from The Warm Company.

Page 94: Floating Frames—
Krakow fabric collection by
Mark Lipinski for Northcott,
and Nature-Fil Bamboo batting
from Fairfield Processing.

**Page 126: Polka Dots &
Paisleys—**Moda fabrics, Warm
& Natural cotton batting from
The Warm Company, and
Master Piece 45 ruler and Static
Stickers.

Page 129: Alternating Stars—
Black is Back fabric collection
from Fabri-Quilt Inc. Machine-
quilted by Amy Shannon.

Page 132: Oak Lodge—
Homespun fabrics from
Diamond Textiles, and
80/20 batting from Fairfield
Processing. Machine-quilted by
Doreen Clink.

Page 140: Shadow Circles—
Formosa by Heidi Dobrott
and Imperial Collection 5
fabric collections from Robert
Kaufman Fabrics, and Nature-
Fil Bamboo batting from
Fairfield Processing.

Page 144: Friendship Forest—
Thermore batting from Hobbs.

Page 153: Pinwheel Daze—
Clowning Around fabric
collection from Wilmington
Prints, and Nature-Fil Bamboo
batting from Fairfield
Processing.

Page 156: Star of My Heart—
Thermore batting from Hobbs.

Page 161: Playing Jacks—
Thermore batting from Hobbs.

Page 170: Oh Baby!— Rayon
and Blendable cotton thread
from Sulky of America, and
Heirloom Fusible cotton
batting from Hobbs.